CONCILIUM

CONCILIUM 2002/2

THE BODY AND RELIGION

Edited by
Regina Ammicht-Quinn and Elsa Tamez

SCM Press · London

Published by SCM Press, 9–17 St Albans Place, London N1 0NX

Copyright © Stichting Concilium

English translations copyright © 2002 SCM-Canterbury Press Ltd

All rights reserved. No part of this publication may be
reproduced, stored in a retrieval system, or transmitted,
in any form or by any means, electronic, mechanical, photocopying,
recording or otherwise, without the prior written permission of
Stichting Concilium, Erasmusplein 1,
6525 HT Nijmegen, The Netherlands

ISBN 0 334 03068 4

Printed by Biddles Ltd, Guildford and King's Lynn

Concilium Published February, April, June, October
December

Contents

Introduction: The Body and Religion
  REGINA AMMICHT-QUINN and ELSA TAMEZ — 7

I. Phenomenological Investigations

The Perfect Body: Biomedical Utopias
  HILLE HAKER — 9

The Superfluous Body: Utopias of Information and Communication Technology
  KLAUS WIEGERLING — 19

The Cultural Coding of the Male and Female Body
  CHRISTINA VON BRAUN — 29

II. Theological and Historical Reflections

Re-evaluating the Body in Eco-Feminism
  ROSEMARY RADFORD RUETHER — 41

The World as God's Body
  SALLY MCFAGUE — 50

Dichotomy or Union of Soul and Body? The Origins of the Ambivalence of Christianity to the Body
  JEAN-GUY NADEAU — 57

Corporeality and Mysticism
  TINA BEATTIE — 66

The Immobile Dance: The Body and the Bible in Latin America
NANCY CARDOSO PEREIRA　　　　　　　　　　　　　　76

Cosmos – Church – Body: Observations on the Notion of
'Healing Pastoral Work'
RAINER BUCHER　　　　　　　　　　　　　　　　　84

III. Intercultural Experiences

The Western Understanding of the Body as a Global Perspective
FARIDEH AKASHE-BÖHME　　　　　　　　　　　　　97

Bodies and Gender in Mesoamerican Religions
SILVIA MARCOS　　　　　　　　　　　　　　　　102

Embodiment and Connexity: An African Purview
GOSBERT T. M. BYAMUNGU　　　　　　　　　　　113

Suffering, Resisting, Healing: An Asian View of the Body
SHARON A. BONG　　　　　　　　　　　　　　　122

Mixed-Race Body, Cosmic Race
CARMIÑA NAVIA VELASCO　　　　　　　　　　　130

Contributors　　　　　　　　　　　　　　　　　　136

Introduction: The Body and Religion

REGINA AMMICHT-QUINN AND ELSA TAMEZ

The globalized world also produces globalized images: globalized images of men and women, and globalized images of human bodies. The break which runs through the world becomes visible in these images of bodies. It is a break which does not simply separate 'us' from 'the others', but time and again also runs through individuals.

On the one hand there are the images of the perfect body, produced by a lifestyle – predominantly, but not only, in the Western industrial nations – which puts a preoccupation with the body at the centre and regards the body as acceptable only if it conforms to clear norms. And on the other hand there are the images of the emaciated, injured, tortured and broken body which come to us – predominantly, but not only – from the impoverished countries and crisis areas of this world. The images could not be more different: here the models in advertisements whose perfect bodies become the criteria for beauty, happiness and salvation, and there the destroyed bodies in whose wretchedness pain, humiliation and death become visible. It is a bitter irony that both the richest and the poorest bodies are often painfully thin and exposed to the danger of perishing from lack of nourishment.

In recent years people have become increasingly aware that our perception of the body, whatever it may be, is not simply 'natural', but has its roots deep in culture. Nevertheless the most elementary bonds between human beings become evident in the basic outlines of corporeality – being born and dying, growing and flourishing, the desires of the body and its pains. Thus for all their diversity the images of the body in the globalized world are not images which stand in unconnected juxtaposition; they are double images in which the shadows of the other images are always visible.

Whereas all over the world the questions of hunger, sickness, persecution, oppression and migration are far from having been solved, above all in the Western industrial nations attitudes towards the body have clearly changed: the body is no longer a fate but the result of actions. Here the body as a whole – and not just its genitalia – becomes a moral problem. In becoming the result of actions, the body gets established as a project. This project of the body aims at perfection – the perfect design for a body which is striven for not only in the media and the beauty industry, but also in the research and health industry.

For a long time Christianity and theology have practised restraint in the interpretation, criticism and active transformation of these twofold globalized images of the body. This may be because Christianity has its own difficult history with the body. For a long time the spiritualizing and the control of everything material was central to the history of Christian piety. The body itself was above all the tangible and perceptible place of human sinfulness, exposed to the drives and an obstacle on the way to salvation.

Today, however, we are in a situation in which more and more frequently concern with the body becomes the cult of the body, and the body is worshipped and sacrificed to in the hope that this will bring salvation. Whereas for some people the possibility of shaping the body becomes central, for others its vulnerability remains at the centre. The awareness of how much shaping the body can damage it and how emphatically its vulnerability shapes it has not yet developed sufficiently.

However, one thing has become clear. Over and above the discussion of sin and control, the body has become an important theme of Christian theology and spirituality. It is urgently necessary for theology critically and in full self-awareness to become involved in current discussions about the body and current practices relating to the body, which are often destructive. Here three things are needed. First, an accurate perception of what is happening, the development of a distinctive hermeneutic which allows a clear theological understanding of contemporary, global and also secular reality; secondly, a self-critical grappling on the part of theology with its own history, in which often both biblical elements of a way of thinking bound up with the body and even the idea of incarnation itself are exploited to promote hostility and contempt for the body; and thirdly, the utopian strength to make the rich Christian tradition fruitful for the present. This issue of *Concilium* seeks to contribute to this development.

The editors are grateful to the following colleagues for criticism, suggestions and support in the conception of this issue: Marcella Althaus-Reid, Nedjelko Ancic, María Pilar Aquino Vargas, José Argüello, Wanda Deifelt, Klaus Demmer, Karl Derksen, Felisa Elizondo, Rosino Gibellini, Thomas Groome, Mary Hunt, Maureen Junker-Kenny, Ursula King, Hubert Lepargneur, Hedwig Meyer-Wilmes, Jean-Guy Nadeau, Edward Schillebeeckx, Donna Singles, Paulo Suess, Christoph Theobald.

I. Phenomenological Investigations

The Perfect Body: Biomedical Utopias

HILLE HAKER

Introduction

Two motifs run through more recent developments in biomedicine: one is the motif of *control* of the body and its functions; the other is that of the active *shaping* of bodily processes at the level of molecular biology and genetics, or even at the organic level, viz. in physiognomy. Now there may be a dispute as to whether the motifs of the control and shaping of the body, which in any case also represent goals, are really utopias, or whether they are not the obsessive ideas of researchers deeply moulded by the history of Western science, who are unwilling to accept the finitude of human beings and therefore also feel that any apparently 'natural' limit is a challenge to research as a whole. But in the self-understanding of those engaged in biomedical and genetic research these goals have positive connotations, so it is worth looking at precisely what they mean.

> If we don't play God, who will? I haven't seen God intervene in anyone's life. People pray to God to prevent tragedies. Right now, in the sense that there are personal genetic tragedies, scientists have the ability to affect the outcome.[1]

Amusement at the style which characterizes the hybrid self-assessments of those involved in genetic research rapidly gives way to horror if we consider the assumptions underlying their aims. At a distance from the specific trends of research these become clear.

I. 'The central dogma of genetics' and the twofold reduction of biotechnology

When biomedics have the human 'body' in view, they focus above all on that aspect which has the connotations of sickness, fragility, and perhaps also ugliness. The body of a severely handicapped child which contradicts not only notions of health but likewise (or even more) normal notions of beauty, represents a threat, whereas the eternally young and therefore apparently immortal body which has been improved genetically, bio-chemically or by hormones, seems attractive. The sick or aged body contradicts the social fetish, i.e. the youthful ideal of a culture of the body which sees the body not as the manifestation of the individuality and history of a person but as an instrument of power which is used in action. However, the greatest control over the human body and the greatest possibility of shaping it now no longer lie on the surface, as it were on the skin, but under the skin, in the specific selection of characteristics and in genetic programming. For this reason it is no coincidence that the beginning of life and, in at least a more prominent way, the end of life are at the centre of the efforts of biomedics working with human genetics.

However, the specifically biomedical way of dealing with the human body has succumbed to a twofold reduction. It no longer perceives the body in the real sense but rather de-corporealizes the body by reducing it to its material nature, to the pure *res extensa* (to use Descartes' term). The materiality of matter with which researchers deal is thus removed from its context of living in the world, namely the body as the manifestation, the expression and medium of the perception of the self and others. Any association with corporeality, the 'non-instrumental relationships with one's own body' and the experience of the body is thus stopped from the start.[2]

Biomedicine is concerned with the body in a fragmented form: organs, tissues, cells and chromosomes. Granted, genes stand as *pars pro toto* for the body, the functions of which are to be understood and which is to be changed, but this is body no longer considered as a whole. What Crick has called 'the central dogma of genetics' is of great significance for the more recent history of genetic research. Although today this 'dogma' can be regarded as a failure at the scholarly level, it continues undiminished to have an influence at the practical level. Here the origin of life is derived from the 'letters' of the 'book of life': 'DNA makes RNA, RNA makes proteins, and proteins make us.'[3]

With such statements genetic research is basing itself on assumptions which are highly controversial in scientific theory generally. As Martin

Altmeyer has demonstrated, it ignores the questions raised by the simple theory of causality, which have led to the development of system theory and chaos research and which show that attention must be paid to the self-organization of organisms and to the compensation of physical processes at other different levels. Emergence, the origin of the new, also cannot be explained with simple genetics, with the central dogma of genetics.

> If the effect were potentially always already present in the cause which generated it, in other words if we had the development of an innate feature, nothing new could emerge. There would be no room for emergence, which is what ontogenesis is about.[4]

What is suggested in the dogma 'one gene, one effect' is history as it were read forwards:

> Almost every cell in our body has a complete set of genes, and this chemical programme determines the change of matter, the growth of the individual cells and their interaction with neighbouring cells.[5]

But in fact genetic research reads the history of the body backwards in precisely the same way as other non-materialistic histories of the body. A conclusion is drawn from the phenotype, say of a child or an adult with Down's Syndrome, to the genotype, and this in turn, in the happy instance of locating relevant characteristics at the levels of the chromosome or gene, can give information about the development of further phenotypes.[6]

Because the early scientific assumptions of genome research can today be taken to have been refuted, genetic research now is far removed from scientific statements about the way in which the genome functions. Such research is therefore also a long way from understanding the way in which the body functions, and understanding its changes. Rather, it is becoming increasingly clear that particularly reflection on the character of the genome as a model – which essentially consists in the analogy between biological systems and computers – shows up the limitations of science. This form of materialization which at the same time de-corporealizes may be scientifically illuminating, but especially the statements in human genetics about the development of illnesses and handicaps are ultimately aimed at a *practical* understanding of ourselves, a self-understanding which is not stamped only by materiality but by the interplay of 'body and spirit' and by the experience of the body.

As a first result we can state that biomedicine dissolves the body as a whole along with the body as a factor of the experience and perception of the self by the human being, whose complement is to be seen in the body. Biological processes are abstracted from the body, but this abstraction is not reversed at the end of the chain of action.

But what utopias emerge in biomedicine? Here the most far-reaching biomedical utopia of the perfect body starts at the beginning of life, but it also extends into old age.

II. Biomedical intervention at the beginning of human life

1. *The donation of nuclei*

At the beginning of human life we are nowadays in the position of being deliberately able to avoid or to encourage particular characteristics. This begins with the selection of the sperm and ova, which are donated within reproductive medicine. In contrast to the context of transplantation medicine, the donation of nuclei is not linked with poverty but is more a phenomenon of the middle or upper class: donations are sought (and found!) from young, usually white, men and women with the highest possible level of education. Potential recipient couples can get very detailed information about donors and can make a choice in accordance with their wishes. Here it is easy to see how the 'central dogma of genetics' has an almost unbroken influence on practice, to the degree that the starting point is a genetic determinism which no one would any longer take seriously at a basic level. The utopia of perfection, the control and shaping not only of human life but of human beings, is the undercurrent here, and it is encouraged by the relevant clinics, which have a commercial interest. The well-known sperm banks of various Nobel prize-winners are enlarged by donors with above average intelligence quotients whose physical characteristics are associated with dominance. Often undisguised racist thinking is expressed in these commercialized branches of reproductive medicine.

2. *Genetic diagnosis*

But there are plenty of possibilities of intervention for biomedicine beyond the donation of nuclei, for example in preserving the distinctive 'genetic condition' of a couple. Thus it is possible to select the sex of a child before pregnancy, a practice which in Western countries so far has been limited to genetic characteristic of sickness which are gender-conditioned, but which is increasingly being used as an element of family planning. In countries with a patriarchal structure the selection of gender before and during pregnancy is being used as a means of combating poverty; sometimes it is even the only possibility of avoiding a threat to existence. Where girls represent a risk of poverty, the selection of sex is by no means gender-neutral and is often even propagated actively by women. By contrast, in Western countries girls are often actually wanted. It is easy to see how social norms can be realized in and with biomedicine.

A distinction has to be made between two spheres of such norms. First, there are possibilities of intervention within a narrower understanding of biomedicine limited to illness and handicap. Thus by means of pre-implantation diagnosis or pre-natal diagnosis it is possible to detect the carriers of characteristics of illnesses, even when these characteristics do not cause the illness in the carriers themselves. We are in a position – or think that we are in a position – to diagnose *in vitro*, i.e. even before the beginning of a pregnancy, dispositions towards the development of breast cancer, skin cancer and certain heart diseases. Embryos which display such a predisposition are destroyed. There are already DNA chips that will certainly be improved further in coming years, on which a variety of genetic characteristics can be stored and then be called up again. Geneticists who are developing these tests are usually biologists or physicians, but they are involved in research and not in the clinical care of patients. Nevertheless – under the flag of reproductive autonomy – the decision about dealing with the genetic knowledge is left to the couples and to patients who want assistance in procreation. Here it is forgotten that, or no mention is made of the fact that, at this point of decision the decisive moves have already been made: the distinction between sickness and health at the level of molecular biology leads almost automatically to couples accepting tests and, of course, also agreeing to the rejection of those embryos which have been classified as genetically 'inferior'. Were there not the assumption of monocausality between gene and development, we would not attach such tremendous importance to the genetic state of a single cell at the beginning of the development. Rather, we would ask about the interplay with proteins, and later about many other factors, including social factors, which extend far beyond the biological context. We would ask about biological and social compensations for particular genetic characteristics. But because a hidden genetic determinism is at work, and because this works as a myth which is seductive or threatening, depending on the context, as a kind of ossified meaning which has become nature in Roland Barthes' sense, the selective actions follow directly from the genetic analyses.

Secondly, the selection of gender represents the norm which is not orientated on the paradigm of health but on the non-medical notions of characteristics of descendants. Thus even now one aim of pre-implantation diagnosis is seen as selecting an embryo in respect of its characteristics as a possible tissue or organ donor for brothers and sisters who have already been born.

3. Germline therapy and genetic enhancement

Not only has diagnosis, followed by selection or rejection and positive choice, become possible; a deliberate alteration of the genetic condition is one of the fields of practice which is now being worked on. This is so-called germline change, sometimes also called germline therapy. Here too there is the narrower biomedical aim of the 'final' removal of genetic characteristics of sickness which have caused suffering in a family for generations, and the further aim of change in the sense of deliberate improvement beyond the characteristics of sickness or handicap. This genetic enhancement may perhaps have previously been ruled out. Nevertheless, such an intervention is in line not only with the technical possibilities but also with a monocausal genetic dogma and a culture which instumentalizes the body and – in areas ranging from genetic equipment to the design of the body – subjects it to norms which show clear traces of violence.

4. The use of embryonic cells by others

If we talk of the biomedical utopias at the beginning of human life we must also note that embryos in the biological sense can provide useful cell material which can serve in the future for medical treatment in the context of tissue and organ transplantation. By contrast, in the context of stem cell research the thought is not of the 'manufacture' of human beings as tissue donors; here so-called superfluous embryos or specially produced embryos are used exclusively for acquiring stem cells and are destroyed in the process. Their further cultivation or development is not technically possible, nor is it intended. This total instrumentalization of embryos also shows a form of biomedicine which on the one hand may not be content with the imperfect and precisely because it has unlimited aims is in search of unusual ways of perfecting biomedicine which violate taboos, though on the other hand the actions involved cannot be perceived as such violations of taboos because of the materialistic presuppositions of the methods. Here too the social norms are present which lead beyond the sickness or characteristics under investigation towards an increasingly strong stigmatization of the human beings involved.

III. The expulsion of the human being from matter

In pre-implantation diagnosis, statements about development are made on the basis of one or two cells taken from an embryo. Now in traditional medicine the prognoses about the possible course of a human life relate to a patient or a client who of course *exists*, a man or a woman who has a body, the processes of which are diagnosed. But in the case of the genetic diagnosis of an embryo the scientists not only deny the cluster of cells that they have taken for biopsy this specific human mode of corporeality; in addition, they also deny that it belongs to the human species, at least in the sense of its moral relevance. Thus the totipotent embryonic cells have no place to belong to existentially or morally; they are u-topian in a new sense. Biologically their place is between a nucleus and a body cell. This intermediate state raises many questions: does the fact that the cells of the embryo are totipotent, in other words have the potentiality of developing into human beings, qualify them for a high degree of protection? Is this potentiality to be interpreted solely in biological terms, or is not rather to be seen against the background of our experiential knowledge, which brings before our eyes the irreversible continuity of the development of the embryo? But perhaps we get entangled in irresolvable contradictions only because we have subjected the moral assessment to biological criteria. Surely a human life cannot be assessed morally in accordance with the criterion of its biological capacities and its state of development? Here at the latest the twofold reduction of the relationship of human beings to their bodies and of corporeality to materiality becomes a case for moral judgment. Moral judgment cannot be abstracted from the *context* of the gene and from biological characteristics generally, any more than it can reduce human beings to their biological characteristics.

Now at the beginning of life there is the problem that human beings have no experience of being in the body because the consciousness is not yet developed. But it is our experience of being in the body, arising from a continuity in our development, which cannot be fragmented. In so far as our relationship to ourselves is of a bodily kind, and in its corporeality is historical, the beginning of human life, which is so removed from our consciousness and our memory, is a limit, just as death is also inaccessible to our consciousness. This limit, though, which is necessary for the constitution of the self, does not lie outside the self, but is rooted in the concept of the self as beginning and end.

In the biomedical model, cells from the embryo are nothing more than biological material which – if all goes well – is subjected to the active control of research. The life sciences are put in quite a different category from the humanities, which in their traditional character recall a past time. Today it no longer seems possible to mediate between these two paradigms within science, nor is such a mediation seen to be necessary by the life sciences. Ethics, too, falls under the verdict of the 'superfluous' or the 'additional', which is also subject to the pressure of social acceptance (on which not least the means for advancement or legal conditions depend). In reflection on the good life it is in no way perceived as an alternative. In this way it becomes clear that the perfect body which is striven for in biomedicine as an implicit or even an explicit utopia is an ideology which has immunized itself against questioning. It can be unmasked as an ideology only through a radical change in perspective, from biology to philosophical anthropology, and from anthropotechnology to a 'creativity of action'.[7]

IV. The ageless society

Biomedicine not only intervenes in the biological processes at the beginning of life, but also embraces almost all the spheres of life. However, after the beginning of life it is above all interested in the end of life. But in contrast to clinical medicine biomedicine is not concerned with questions about help in dying or the quality of life in old age, but rather in the question of the aging and dying of cells.[8] If the drosophila fly is of immeasurable importance for the genome problem, the threadworm has become the model for aging after the success achieved in the middle of the 1990s in stopping the aging process of this worm. For some years now, biomedical research has been on the offensive in this sphere. Thus the American Academy of Anti-Aging Medicine, which by its own account has more than 8,000 members, describes its mission as follows:

> The American Academy of Anti-Aging Medicine promotes the development of technologies, pharmaceuticals, and processes that retard, reverse, or suspend the deterioration of the human body resulting from the physiology of aging, and provides continuing medical education for physicians.[9]

Interestingly, 90% of the membership is drawn from physicians or researchers in the sphere of health. The sponsors of this important movement are also worth mentioning: in addition to an Alzheimer Prevention Organization these are some biotechnological enterprises, but also universities which carry on biomedical research (Harvard University, Manchester University), or the International Olympic Committee. The organization is aiming at a 'new', ageless society with a life-span of up to 150 years and reproductive cloning as an ingredient of immortality. It is no coincidence that here, in the cloning of human beings, biomedicine and gene technology at the beginning of life meet up with biomedicine at the end of life.

Because these and similar notions like the utopia of the perfect body inherent in biomedicine are influential, it is necessary to grapple with the image and myths which emerge in them. One means of grappling with them is to analyse the images and the constructions of the body and the threat which seems to be posed by the body living in the world and its bodily experience. Here it is necessary to evaluate the practical effect of 'the central dogma of genetics', despite its theoretical failure. Ethics must be concerned with re-transferring the images of perfection into their social context. Then it could prove that a 'good life' need not necessarily be identified with the immortality of one's own gene, that finitude, corporeality and mortality have values of their own, and that the twofold reduction of the human being to the body and the body to biological matter comes at a price which we are not prepared to pay – or at any rate, for the sake of our own selves, must not be ready to pay. This is the price of humanity in the sense of normative equality under the condition of individual difference; it is the price of human dignity.

Translated by John Bowden

Notes

1. James Watson, quoted in A.Petersen, 'Biofantasies: genetics and medicine in the print news media', *Social Science and Medicine* 52, 2001, pp.1255–68: 1255.
2. For detail see A. Barkhaus, 'Körper und Identität: Vorüberlegungen zu einer Phänomenologie des eigensinnigen Körpers', in S. Jaross and L. Welzin, *Tanz Politiik Identität*, Hamburg 2001, pp.17–51. I am grateful to A. Barkhaus for drawing my attention to this article.
3. Quoted by Evelyn Fox Keller, *The Century of the Gene*, London 2000, p.76.
4. M. Altmeyer, 'Im Geschosshagel der Sequenzieroboter. Der neue Scientismus ignoriert die Ergebnisse der modernen Wissenschaftsthorie', *Frankfurter Rundschau*, 22 May 2001.
5. F. Crick, *What Mad Pursuit. A Personal View of Scientific Discovery*, London and New York 1988, quoted in S. Graumann, *Die somatische Gentherapie. Entwicklung und Anwendung aus ethischer Sicht*, 2000, pp.92–121. Graumann sets the central dogma of genetics against the background of alternative possibilities of interpretation and criticisms. Cf. also Fox Keller, *Century of the Gene* (n.3).
6. For details U. Wolf, 'The genetic contribution to the phenotype', *Human Genetics* 95, 1995, pp.127–48, is still very important.

7. H. Joas, *Die Kreativität des Handelns*, Frankfurt am Main 1992.
8. P. A. Möller (ed.), *Die Kunst des Älterns. Medizinethische Diskurse über den Älterungsprozess in exogener Einflussnahme*, Frankfurt am Main 2001.
9. Cf. the relevant information on http//www.worldhealth.net/a4m/overview.html.

The Superfluous Body: Utopias of Information and Communication Technology

KLAUS WIEGERLING

When two aircraft flew into the World Trade Centre on 11 September 2001,very few people thought of how at the moment of impact bodies were being shattered and burned. It all looked as unreal as a Hollywood film, When from a distance one saw people escaping the inferno by leaping from a great height in final desperation, one had in mind images of great stunts. And even the collapse of the two tremendous towers could have been a scene from Emerich's *Independence Day*. From a distance the horror seemed as awe-inspiring as the painting of a battle, and only one's mind told one what was happening. Even in what is perhaps the most virtual region of the globe, at the symbolic centre of economic power, people were dying in large numbers and 'physically'. We can be certain that this terrible experience will bring with it a further development of media technological utopias which try to overcome the vulnerable human body, under deadly threat, this vehicle which leads to death.

Introduction: the body – a key theme

Since the 1980s the body has been a key theme, and not only in the context of discussions about information and communication theory. At present the body is considered above all from two perspectives. First there is interest in the physiological determination of human beings, which is the theme of the debate over gene technology and biopolitics. And secondly there is interest in the volatilizing of the body in the way in which the media accelerate our lives, the way in which the body is dissolved as information in cyberspace.

In the debate over both gene and media technology, schemes are put forward which move away from the guidelines of the experiential sciences. In these schemes a clear division between 'science' and 'science fiction' is no longer possible. Regardless of how we assess such theoretical schemes, there is no disputing the fact that they are having effects on scientific policy, the self-understanding of various disciplines, and not least on human self-understanding. To this degree a concern with the utopias of information and communication technology is not only a contribution towards diagnosing a dominant way of understanding science and technology which is strongly stamped by neo-positivist and utilitarian naivety, but also a contribution to diagnosing the spirit of the time.

In the discussion on the body it is possible not only to identify the ongoing expression of Puritan ideologies but also to establish a loss in orientation deriving from a technologized understanding of the world which detaches the question of what can be done from the question of responsibility or leaves this question to other 'weaker' (as they are often termed) authorities like religion or philosophy. The loss of the body is an analogue to the loss of cultural ties, and thus the expression of a loss of value, for the body is by no means just a physiological entity; it has been formed and is formed culturally, and we cannot have a neutral relationship with it.

Now why do voices keep being raised, especially in the so-called cyber-community, in a demand to overcome the body? First we must attempt to clarify what the body means and how our notion of it is changing under the influence of the media.

I. What is the body?

The body is the only entity in the world which can be guided directly by our consciousness. The body is thought of as a psycho-physical entity. Through it, as a part of the world, and its capacities, we have a direct access to the world, though only from a particular perspective.

1. Constantly present

The body is constantly present, but only by way of exception and in perspective is it the object of our intentional life. On the one hand its presence is not anonymous, but on the other hand it is not given in the mode of an explicit content of consciousness. The presence of the body is expressed in moods and dispositions which accompany the content of our consciousness. Thus the body is a pre-conceptual presence which accompanies all our intentional entanglements in the world. By means of the body we take part in a shared world. We are a natural element of it and can fix ourselves and this world in a particular perspective.

As distinct from bodies which are thought to be inanimate, the body is marked out by a reference to itself. According to Kant, our bodily capacities make it possible for us to encounter the world. These capacities, which can be summed up under the term sensuality, are the condition of all knowledge, but also its limit, in so far as all knowledge that is regarded as objective must be restricted to the conditions of sensuality. The capacity of sensuality is the organ for the contingent and the subjective; the capacity of the mind is the organ for the universal and objective. But sensuality is by no means just a capacity which mediates the world and stands at the service of knowledge. In his *Anthropology* Kant goes at length into the body's self-reference. The provocation of the senses stimulates, gives pleasure, and leads to the satisfaction of sensual tendencies. Thus sensuality is a capacity which exerts pressure towards provocation. This pressure is exercised in unconscious reflexes, in other words drives. 'The more strongly the senses . . . feel themselves affected,' writes Kant, 'the less they learn. Conversely, if they are to learn much they must have moderate affections. In the strongest light one sees nothing . . .'[1] The self-reference of the body is also the basis for the mistrust of it. The body not only leads to the world but also leads out of it. Its self-reference not only bewitches the mind but is also directed against its own functionality. Those who listen to music which is too loud damage their hearing. Since Plato's remarks in his dialogue *Cratylus*,[2] in which the body is described as the prison of the soul, in a variety of philosophical and ideological traditions there has time and again been emphasis on the limitations and the dysfunctionality of the body.

2. *Individuality*

The body is an expression of my individuality. Thanks to our bodies, we occupy a concrete place in space and time. For this reason, in mediaeval angelology the disembodied angels, who were nevertheless also created, were not regarded as individuals but as a genre. Disembodied light figures could not be located in space. By the spatial and temporal positioning of our psycho-physical existence and its kinaesthetic and locomotive capacities, we achieve what we call orientation. The body not only gives us position but also orientates us. Through it we can approach ourselves as specific bodies and also distance ourselves from them; through it we can understand the phenomenon of right- or left-handedness, and positions in space make sense only in the light of the positions of our bodies.

As a psycho-physical entity the body has not only a genetic but also a cultural disposition. Particular capacities have a cultural advantage and are developed accordingly. There are advantages in seeing, hearing, touching and tasting which are articulated in different bodily forms. As early as the nineteenth century the biologists Hering and Semon developed a theory of the mneme, in which they attempted to show that the memory not only belongs to the sphere of consciousness but is already a basic property of organic matter.[3] All animate being has a history which distinguishes it from dead matter. This earlier impression has been preserved, even if its causes have ceased to exist. Any stimulus leaves behind a physiological trace, an 'engram'. This determines how the organism will respond to similar stimuli in the future. Thus all reactions are dependent not only on the present state of the body, but also on the totality of the influences which have been exerted on it. Now the sum of these stimuli reproduces a special cultural disposition in so far as they work on our bodies from a specific cultural area. The environment which provides stimuli differs from age to age and from region to region. Husserl designated the body the 'zero body',[4] which is bound up with an absolute Here. Husserl's further designation of the cultural world as a 'zero member'[5] orientated on my personality is more than an analogue. Alien cultural phenomena can be disclosed and understood from this 'zero member'. The body itself is the first expression of culture. Not least, language has a bodily disposition. Aristotle's definition of man as a being that has *logos*, i.e. can speak, cannot be thought of apart from the body. This relationship, too, is clarified by mediaeval angelology. Communication between angels does not take place in language and discourse, but intuitively.

3. Boundary

The body functions as a boundary between the indirect and the direct. It is directly bound up with my psyche and my habits, and at the same time it is the medium which associates me with what I am not. Cassirer defined the body as the primal phenomenon of mediality, as 'the first model and pattern for a symbolic relationship'.[6] Merleau-Ponty regards the bodily capacities as an expression of the body's 'being in the world' which transcend its current capacities. He describes this phenomenon by citing phantom members: 'What . . . rejects the mutilation and breaking is the self which is engaged in a physical and interpersonal world, which despite all the lack produced by amputation continues to be pulled towards the world, and which to this degree does not recognize *de jure* either amputation or lack. The failure to acknowledge lack is merely the other side of the way in which we belong to the world . . . To have a phantom arm, to remain open for all the action of which alone the arm is capable, is to preserve the practical field that was possessed before the mutilation. The body is the vehicle of being in the world, and to have a body means . . . to identify oneself with certain plans and constantly to be involved in them.'7

II. A change of conception

The relation to the body determines many forms of life. In almost all cultures asceticism and the suppression of desires are regarded as a contribution to cultural refinement. Etiquette and rituals organize physical proximity. Here our notion of the body is to an important degree governed by the conditions of the media. The historical tendency in our conceptions of the body can be summed up under the slogan 'from communion to communication'. The body itself is the first medium which relates to the world. At the beginning of humankind, interpersonal relations largely took place in an area which coincided with our field of vision, our range of hearing, the distance we could call, what we could sense and what we could touch. In the community (*communio*) there is a direct involvement, and proximity is produced by bodily contact which becomes as intimate as the act of sex. *Communio* is originally the notion of bodies united in a fellowship bound together by blood.

The first great change in conceptions of the body was articulated in the way in which it was depicted. This brought a greater awareness of the typological, and what was absent in time and space was given a symbolic presence. We can see a scepticism about naturalistic portrayals even in the earliest forms of artistic expression. Naturalistic depictions often disclose weaknesses, and make disharmony and ugliness visible. Stylization, exaggeration and transformation quickly become the ingredients of artistic creation. A pictorial depiction is meant to cause excitement, to call for humility, to banish the baneful; it is aimed at having an effect over and above the presence of the absent.

1. Writing

With writing, a historical element which bursts open the present finds its way into human exchange. The *communio* which is based on direct exchanges between bodies is replaced by a communication based on writing. Assuming a bodily distance is a presupposition of communication. Conceptions of the body become more abstract in cultures dominated by writing. In religious contexts bodies become symbolic embodiments. Dietmar Kamper writes that 'this regularity becomes striking in the *sensus communis*, in the exclusive metaphor of a particular body which is situated in the middle, between "communion" and "communication". This is the "radiant body of the god", that embodiment of the symbolic order of the West in which an intersection of matter and spirit, flesh and word, has become possible."[8]

2. Media society

With the dominance of written codings, a move away from the visible world and from the body takes place. The medium of writing above all covers the structural realm, i.e. things which lie below the visible surface. Right at the beginning of the last century, Balázs pointed out that with the victorious progress of written expressions, visible expressions of the spirit in gestures and mimes faded into the background.[9] The Reformation reinforced this move away from the world that can be grasped by the senses. Finally, developments in the late nineteenth and the twentieth century have been stamped by the pictorial depictions in photography and the cinema. On the one hand here the body has been naturalized; on the other it has been subjected to intensified norms. Models and film stars are matrices of fashionable ideals which are replaced in rapid succession. There is a tendency to make the body superficial. The body becomes an object to be shaped. We can impose our wills on it, and hand it over to surgeons and trainers to shape. Ways of deliberately shaping the body to make it more powerful or to transcend it in religious practices become forms of body-styling. The body is now a piece of matter that can be shaped, a body which is attached to a person but is not a psychophysical entity. Human beings are as it were forced out of their own body, and stand in a mirror relationship to them.

Baudrillard further reinforces this notion when he asserts that the progressive media society is in a video stadium in which people experience themselves as refractions and reproductions of themselves.[10] In this infinite refraction we no longer perceive ourselves as erotic beings but as pornographic beings, i.e. no longer as totalities but as split up into bodily details and mechanized bodily functions. Whereas the erotic cannot be thought of without a soul, pornography needs no soul. The pornographic attitude is enough for the soul-less body, which can be exchanged at any time.

Lastly, informational codings make it possible to detach pictorial depictions completely from individual representations. We no longer need actors for animated films or computed games. Bodies are shaped by ideal measurements which are arrived at statistically. The whole creature is composed of exchangeable elements which can be combined at random, from the voice to the skin colour. What remains is the analogy of these creatures, behind which we cannot go.

3. Cyborg

The science-fiction cyborg can stand as a symbol of the transitional form of the advanced media society, a form which is slowly taking leave of the body. The cyborg is a machine made of mechanical and organic material, equipped with the informational capacities of a big computer. Bodily the cyborg is still in the world, but its existence is only conditionally tied up with particular hardware. Its intellectual capacities can be transferred at any time to another media vehicle. Figures like the automated killer T-1000 in Cameron's film *Terminator 2* change their hardware, but their purpose remains the same. In such science-fiction material, changes in our understanding of the body can be seen which are also to be found in science. Thus the biological hardware of human beings is seen as being too vulnerable to survive coming environmental catastrophes.

The increasing media treatment of the body can also be seen not least in preparations for the showing of the exhibition *Corporeal Worlds*, which began in Germany and has been shown in many countries. The corpses exhibited, which were prepared by the Heidelberg pathologist Günther von Hagen, serve an exclusively aesthetic end, not anatomical instruction. On the exhibition's website, *Corporeal Worlds* is described as the 'anatomical theatre of modernity'. So this is a media presentation. And what happens here to the corpse corresponds precisely to the basic idea of presentations on the mass media; the most private and most intimate is exposed to the public gaze.

III. Overcoming the body?

The desire to overcome our bodily state is not an invention of the age of modern information technologies and communication technologies. The body is an expression of irreversible processes of ageing which can be experienced directly. They are an expression of our vulnerability and the limitations of our will. Nowhere is our being towards death more visible than in the decay of our bodies. Thus the wish to overcome the conditions of the body is at the same time a wish for total freedom. If we cannot become gods, could we at least become angels who exist without bodies and without pain? And the Faustian dream of unlimited knowledge has a fascination of its own.

1. The utopia of total freedom

First of all it is a matter of replacing the body with other hardware. Entry into cyberspace is prepared for by a kind of crippling of bodily resources. 'Entry into cyberspace,' writes Rötzer, 'will further accentuate the behavioural characteristics of a highly technologized society, namely sitting, standing and lying, because the body will increasingly become a burdensome attachment.'[11]

However, one problem of these modern information utopias remains the fact that even the dream of cyber-existence is not a logical one, in bits and bytes. Cyber-existence is not an informational operator. Bodies must also come into being in cyberspace, even if the action there is virtual. The digital dreaming of our day transfers bodies and bodily properties into the immaterial realm, but it does not do away with them. Cyberspace is still a sphere of symbols and analogies which cannot be thought of without reference to the senses, or without reference to bodily objects. Even the descriptions of such utopias by spokesmen of the cyber-community like Hans Moravec remain vague: 'Beyond the earth extends the boundless world of space: a good arena for a tremendous growth in any bodily and mental dimension.'[12] No limits can put a brake on the expansionary drive of the new being which populates cyberspace. But even there, the law of selection and competition prevails. For Moravec the principle of self-improvement replaces procreation: 'Living beings will no longer be defined by their bodily and geographical limits; they will establish, extend and defend identities as transactions of information in cyberspace.'[13] So cyberspace is simply the USA with a West which can be settled in for ever.

Only the laws of the market prevail in this world of immortal and inviolable agents. None of the problems which compel us to engage in ethical reflection, like famines, diseases, the unfair distribution of goods, oppression, etc., exist in the new realm of freedom. However, the question remains of how this market of virtual goods is to exist when bodily needs no longer exist, and desires are no longer stimulated and do not need to be satisfied.

2. Puritanical hatred

The mercantile ingredients of a Puritan ethic are preserved in the bodiless cyber-realm of freedom. Rainer Fischbach describes this state of affairs as follows:

However, only that which can be . . . digitalized and quantified enjoys a supposedly eternal value and thus invulnerability in this order, and that was always the entry ticket to Puritan bliss. People of flesh and blood – wetware in cyber-jargon – will in the end still find themselves in the grip of vulnerable, uncontrollable power. The ideology of cyberspace proves to be a new disguise for the Puritan hatred of the flesh, its theoretical substratum the umpteenth remake of the Manichaean myth. The cyber-community is a further link in the chain of neo-Gnostic sects. Barlow's remark that 'our world ... is not where bodies live' is somehow threatening. His realm of light is in truth an idealist realm of the dead, in which everything is reduced to its digital shadow, and its secret programme is in fact one of destroying the world.[14]

However, Nietzsche's Superman still goes his way in the modern cyber-fantasies. There are no moral restrictions in cyberspace. The individual is dissolved into a knowing something which spends its cyberlife as a player. It can be faded in and out of exchanges without consequences for its life or for the other player. As in games, so in the cyberworld it is possible to fail and break the rules, but there is nothing like guilt and sin. All action in the bodiless realm is inconsequential. Like angels, those who exist in cyberspace need no ethics.

Cyber-ideologists like Barlow and Moravec are spokesmen of a new puritanical spirit. On the one hand their thought remains technological and naïve, but on the other hand it is firmly rooted in the mercantile categories of a Protestant ethic. Their utopian schemes are simply Hollywood fantasies with attempts to ground them in technology.

If a removal from location, time and body are the structural characteristics of the virtual on the Internet, we must ask what effect these structural characteristics have on our bodily life in community. Capurro states that a net ethic must always ask itself what effect digital actions have on the bodily existence of human beings as a community,[15] for Kant already stated that moral laws apply only to 'human beings as beings with a rational nature, who are baneful enough to embark on pleasure but who transgress the moral law which they recognize as soon as they see it, and even if they pursue it, nevertheless do so reluctantly (their inclinations resist it)'.[16]

Making the body superfluous already begins with making conversation superfluous in chat rooms, where the participants act as anonymous and apparently uninvolved players, whose words do not commit them in any way. Although conversation is a primal image of the communicable, even in Plato it needs bodies as its foundation. All practice is grounded in this bodily conditioning and the involvement of those engaged in the exchanges. It is here that the analogue of our thought, which clearly cannot be surpassed, is articulated. Even in cyberspace the new utopian beings act by giving bodies to their thought and to this degree permanently recalling their defects and origins. This overcoming of the bodily is none other than an overcoming of the human itself, none other than flight into the unhistorical, and thus an expression of self-forgetfulness.

Translated by John Bowden

Notes

1. Immanuel Kant, *Anthropologie im pragmatischer Absicht*, in id., *Werkausgabe* XII, ed. W. Weischedel, Frankfurt am Main 1968, p.452.
2. Plato, *Cratylus*, 400c.
3. Cf. Ewald Hering, *Über das Gedächtnis als allgemeine Funktion der organischen Materie*, Vienna 1876; Richard Semon, *Die Mneme*, Leipzig 1904.
4. Edmund Husserl, *Cartesianische Meditationen und Pariser Vorträge*, Husserliana Vol.I, The Hague 1960, p.162.
5. Ibid., p.152.
6. Ernst Cassirer, *Philosophie der symbolischen Formen* III, Darmstadt 1994, p.117 (first published 1929).
7. Maurice Merleau-Ponty, *Phenomenology of Perception*, London 1962, p.106.
8. Dietmar Kamper, 'Poesie, Prosa, Klartext. Von der Kommunion der Körper zur Kommunikation der Maschinen', in H. U. Gumbrecht and K. L. Pfeiffer, *Materialität der Kommunikation*, Frankfurt am Main 1988, p.49.
9. Cf. Bela Balázs, *Der sichtbare Mensch oder Die Kultur des Films*, Vienna and Leipzig 1924.
10. Cf. Jean Baudrillard, 'Videowelt und fraktales Subjekt', in Ars Electronica (ed.), *Philosophien der neuen Technologie*, Berlin 1989.
11. Florian Rötzer, *Digitale Weltentwürfe*, Munich 1998, p.233.
12. Hans Moravec, 'Körper, Roboter, Geist', in S. Iglhaut and F. Rötzer (eds), *Stadt am Netz*, Mannheim 1996, p.105.
13. Ibid., p.109.
14. Rainer Fischbach, 'Der Mythos des 21.Jahrhunderts? Vom Krieg der Sterne zum Cyberspace', *Blätter für deutsche und internationale Politik*, June 1998, p.685.
15. Rafael Capurro, 'Operari sequitur esse – Zur Existential-Ontologischen Begründung der Netzethik', in R. Capurro and T. Hausmanninger (eds), *Netzethik – Konzepte und Konkretionen einer Informationsethik für das Internet*, Munich 2002 (in preparation).
16. Immanuel Kant, *Die Metaphysik der Sitten*, in id., *Werkausgabe* VIII, ed. W. Weischedel, Frankfurt am Main 1968, p. 508.

The Cultural Coding of the Male and Female Body

CHRISTINA VON BRAUN

Every religious and secular community develops particular patterns in accordance with which the individual body is coded. In this way the individual bodies become a reflection of the collective body. In turn this needs the analogy with the individual human body to depict and provide the unity and cohesion of society. The cultural codings appear most clearly from the way in which the bodies of the sexes are 'marked', say, by tattoos or mutilations, and above all by the rules of behaviour imposed on the two sexes – rules which are usually not understood as symbolic assignments, but are taken to be governed by nature or biology. The extinction of the symbolic (which implies a move into 'visible reality') is part of the 'strategy of self-depiction' in the collective body; in order to make people forget that the body is imaginary, this empowers the biological characteristics of the asexual body so that it can itself appear as a 'biological' or a 'natural' body. This reciprocal relationship between the collective and the individual body is one of the reasons why the patterns according to which the biological 'reality' of the sexual body can be 'read' and interpreted from one culture to another are either contradictory or vary to a considerable degree.

In what follows I want to attempt to depict this reciprocal relationship by a comparison of the cultural coding of the bodies of the two sexes in Judaism and Christianity. Precisely because Judaism and Christianity are both religions of the book, and there are therefore similar medial structures for coding in each of them, it is possible to make such a comparison. For just as the medial framework governs the way in which society is formed, so too it shapes the cultural coding of the individual body which society has to reflect.[1] But at the same time the medial conditions of these two 'religions of the book' bring about a very deep distinction between them. That is the case on the one hand with the system of writing and on the other with their relationship to the image. My thesis is that these differences led to different symbolic ordering of the sexes in Judaism and Christianity, which are so deep that one is tempted to ask whether there is such a thing as a 'Jewish' and a 'Christian' sexuality.

I. The system of writing and the symbolic coding of the sexual body

1. Written and oral communication...

The Semitic alphabet was the first alphabet of any kind. It was formed around 1000 BC, about the same time as the first monotheistic religion, the Mosaic faith. The Greek alphabet came into being only around two hundred years later, and it brought in its train the formation of the polis, and democracy with its written law; the development of philosophy and science in the form in which they still stamp the thought of the West – for example as a sharp distinction between religion and reason; the beginning of historical thought and with it thought in terms of utopian models (of social life or scientific progress) which call for implementation. Finally, this system of writing also resulted in a symbolic ordering of the sexes which as it were 'biologizes' the dichotomy of spirit/matter (body) and nature/culture and elevates it to the status of a natural law. The thinking which emerged from the Greek alphabet was later to contribute to the dissemination of Christianity.

The essential difference between the Semitic and the Greek systems of writing lies in the fact that in the Semitic alphabet only the consonants are written, whereas the Greek alphabet contains all the sounds of speech including the vowels, and thus reproduces the spoken word in its complete form. The consonantal alphabet entails that texts written in Semitic writing can be read only by those who also speak the language, i.e. those who can infer from the content what term, what meaning could be intended. This in turn resulted in the establishment in the Jewish religious and secular traditions of a juxtaposition of written and oral communication which was expressed, for example, in the fact that on the one hand holy scripture was fixed – after its publication by Ezra around 440 BC there could be no further change to any words. On the other hand, oral exegesis meant that time and again there was a new exposition and reception of the text. Thus from generation to generation the handing down of holy scripture was done through speaking bodies.

By contrast, the Greek alphabet with its complete covering of spoken language led to competition between written and oral communication. On the one hand this led to a devaluation of the fleeting, spoken word by contrast with the 'eternal' written notion, and on the other hand to a gradual reshaping of spoken language in accordance with the laws and logic of what had been written down. Christ as the 'word made flesh' is *the* symbolic figure of this basic relationship between writing and speech, spirit and matter, and therefore the history of Christian society can also be read as the history of a long historical process in the course of which the spoken word was gradually reordered and reshaped by the written word: this process accelerated tremendously with the invention of printing, and around 1800, in parallel to the beginning of universal literacy, it contributed to the gradual development of the possibility of distinguishing between oral and written communication.

2. . . . in the sexual order

This relationship between written and oral communication is also reflected in the symbolic ordering of the sexes. In both cultural traditions the male body becomes the symbolic form of the written word, whereas the female body represents oral communication. But the interpretation of this relationship is basically different. In the Greek and later Christian tradition, in parallel to the devaluation of oral experience there was a devaluation of female 'fleshliness'. This was in turn followed by a reshaping of 'femininity' in accordance with the laws of logic which corresponds to the reshaping of spoken language in accordance with the laws of scripture. By contrast, the juxtaposition of oral and written communication through the Semitic consonantal alphabet was reflected in a symbolic ordering of the sexes in which the female body, which stands for the vowel, the sign which is not written, points to the 'voids' of the Semitic alphabet, the 'physis which is pushed out'. Oral communication, imagined as feminine, forms the 'sounding body' without which the signs cannot come into the world. The female body is not the symbolic vehicle of revelation – this is inscribed in the signs of scripture and through circumcision these are in turn inscribed on the male body – but the symbolic vehicle for the 'speaking' of revelation, for the 'speaking, oral Torah'. That means that in the Jewish tradition the two symbolic functions – the male body as the symbol-bearer of signs and the female body as the expression of signs – are dependent on each other. The sounds without the signs are insignificant, and conversely the signs can only attain 'significance' through the sounds.

II. Prohibition of images, veneration of images and images of the sexes

The different relationship between oral and written communication becomes evident again in the relationship to the image: the Jewish prohibition of images on the one hand and the Christian veneration of images on the other. Here, too, the medial framework is reflected in the symbolic ordering of the sexes in each religion.

1. Difference and symbiosis

In *Moses and Monotheism* Freud described the overcoming of matriarchy and the origin of the prohibition of images with almost identical words. He claimed that the 'turning from the mother to the father points in addition to a victory of intellectuality over sensuality', in other words cultural progress,[2] and remarked that in the prohibition of images 'a sensory perception was given second place to what may be called an abstract idea – a triumph of intellectuality over sensuality'.[3] However, his identification of image and sensuality gives rise to a paradox. For although there is 'cultural progress' in both the Jewish and the Christian religion (in Freud's sense of a 'turning from the mother to the father'), in the Jewish religion this is combined with the prohibition of images, but in Christianity with the veneration of images. Evidently different things are meant in the two religions by the 'triumph of intellectuality over sensuality', and these differences are reflected in the symbolic ordering of the sexes.

Among other things, the symbolic ordering of the sexes in Judaism is evident from the ritual laws relating to male and female bodies: the difference of the sexes is prescribed with the circumcision of the man and the regulations about menstrual blood. At the same time circumcision also represents a symbolic inscription of the signs of scripture on the male body, to which religion has entrusted control of scripture. The emphasis on the difference between the sexes appears on the one hand as a reflection of the emphasis on the difference between oral and written communication if we identify the latter with intellectuality and the former with sensuality; on the other hand, however, this also reflects the difference between God and human beings. The laws which inscribe the difference between the sexes on bodies and make them visible as cultural codes point to the distinction between the immortality of God and the mortality of 'incomplete' human beings – and the prohibition of images, which forbids both the depiction of God and the perpetuation of the human face, reflects this process.

Central to the Christian ordering of the sexes is an ideal of symbiosis, the abolition of the distinction between the sexes – and this ideal reflects the Christian saving message of a union with God. In both cases the image is of central importance. After the fourth century, with the establishment of the church – for the first time, in parallel to this, images appear in the Christian houses of God[4] – this connection becomes increasingly clear. In contrast to the Old Testament concept of knowledge, which implies the knowledge of human incompleteness in the sexual act itself – 'Adam knew his wife' – the Christian concept of 'knowledge' takes on a significance which shows it to be a synonym for 'identification' in the sense of being identical. Again the image plays an important role in this kind of 'knowledge'.

> In the realm of spirituality or mysticism the fact that human beings are images makes it possible for them to attain to knowledge of God; for like can be known only by like, and knowledge presupposes a certain affinity of being between subject and object . . . Finally, in the state of bliss, according to I John 3.2 similarity and divinization correspond to seeing face to face. Conversely, the contemplation of Christ or God in the soul develops the picture: the changing contemplation likens the beholder to the one who is beheld.[5]

2. Inner and outer person

Such a concept of knowledge, which means 'similarity', 'affinity of being' and 'being in the image of', corresponds to the saving event in the eucharist, in which a transformation of men and women takes place through the 'unifying knowledge' of God – and the symbolic ordering of the sexes again reflects the ideal of 'being in the image'. That is already evident in Paul's statement that the man need not veil his head 'because he is the image and glory of God; but woman is the glory of man'.[6] However, this statement contradicted what is said in Genesis, according to which God created human beings in his image, 'male *and* female'.[7] So Augustine's doctrine of the Trinity developed a new idea of the sexes as being in the image of God, according to which the woman is an image of God only if male and female appear as one being. By herself she cannot be the image of God, since she was created as the image of Adam, whereas even alone the man is an image of God.[8] Thus far his teaching corresponded to that of Paul. But since Augustine also wanted to do justice to what is said in Genesis, he developed the doctrine that the soul is divided into two, comprising an 'inner person' (*homo interior*) and an 'outer person' (*homo exterior*). The outer person is responsible for earthly needs and is feminine; the inner person is responsible for spiritual needs and is male. Since only human beings, of either sex, have both parts of the soul, the female soul therefore also has a *homo interior*, and the woman is also an 'image of God'; however, this is only the case if her body acts in accordance with the male part of the soul. If her body acts in accord with the female part of the soul, the woman is not an image of God.[9]

This idea that the spiritual soul (defined as male) is in the image of God, and the notion derived from it of a creative power of the spiritual over the bodily, formed the basis for the Christian ordering of the sexes, which on the one hand prescribed the differences between the sexes but on the other hand also meant a symbiosis, a unity of the sexes. So if in Judaism the prohibition of images marks the difference between God and human beings, in Christianity the veneration of images and the ideal of union with God are closely connected. That is bound up with the incarnation of God, to which those who argued for the veneration of images appealed. The concept of the 'image' is also closely related to the mystical experience of a union with God in Meister Eckhart:

> I have already often said that no one can separate an image as image and that of which it is an image. If the soul lives in that in which it is the image of God, it gives birth; here lies true union, which cannot separate any creatures (from one another). Despite God himself, despite the angels, despite the souls and all creatures (I say), that they cannot separate the soul, where it is an image of God (from God). That is true union, and herein lies true bliss.[10]

3. Sexuality as becoming one

The union of a spirituality imagined as masculine with the woman as 'image' again reflects the saving message of a union with the blood and body of the Lord. So it is no coincidence that in the testimonies of the mystics, as in Meister Eckhart, the eucharist seems like a description of the sexual act:

> For in it you are kindled and become hot, and in it you are hallowed and bound to and united with him alone. In the sacraments and really nowhere else you find the grace that your bodily forces are so united and brought together by the glorious power of the bodily presence of the body of our Lord that all the scattered senses of man and the disposition are brought together and purified in this ... and being strengthened by his body your body will be renewed. For we are to be changed into it and fully united

with him (cf. II Cor.3.18), so that his becomes ours and all ours, our heart and his one heart, and our body and his one body.[11]

Meister Eckhart's remarks about marriage and love between the sexes make it quite clear that the parallels between love of God and love of the other sex were also quite deliberate. 'Now the nature of love is that it stems from and flows from two as simply one. Never as something twofold: love does not exist as two! Two as one, that is irrefutably and naturally love, full of force and glow and desire.'[12] In other words, the symbolic ordering of the sexes in Christian doctrine 'biologizes' and 'naturalizes' the message of Christianity in such a way that there may be no distinction between the symbol and the 'reality' or the sign of scripture and the body which speaks. If God had 'imagined' earth, as Meister Eckhart puts it, in Christianity an 'imagined gender' developed. This is a concept of sexuality which affirms becoming one, the abolition of duality. Such a concept was contrary to the symbolism of the sexes in Judaism, so the question almost necessarily arose whether these different concepts of the coding of the male and female body did not also result in different concepts of sexuality. Therefore when in what follows I go on to speak about sexuality, I do not mean the sexual act, the cultural coding which gives sexuality itself its 'significance' and which, as Foucault already showed in his *History of Sexuality*, changes from one cultural context to another. Like cultural memory, 'sexuality' (in the collective singular) also has a function in forming the community.

III. Religion and sexuality

1. Judaism: male, but not sexual

Judaism does not know any condemnation of sexuality and sexual satisfaction, of the kind that has dominated Christian thought in many eras and was ultimately only done away with in post-Christian societies when – thanks to a more precise knowledge of the process of procreation – it became possible to think about sexuality and reproduction as independent from each other. David Biale writes laconically in his book *Eros and the Jews* that Judaism awards no medals for celibate behaviour.[13] Sexuality is regarded as part of the human condition; as a condition of procreation it offers the possibility of encountering the sting of death, but at the same time it is also a symptom of human incompleteness and a difference from God. Tykva Frymer-Kensky, lecturer in the Department of Biblical Civilization at the Rabbinical College, writes that the God of Israel is thought of in male terms but not in sexual terms. God is not at all phallic and cannot represent either male virility or sexual potency. Anthropomorphic biblical language uses bodily images of the arm, the right hand, the mouth, but God is never imagined below the waist. God is a-sexual or trans-sexual or meta-sexual, depending on how we consider the phenomenon. God is never sexual.[14]

Nor does God act in a sexual way. Granted, God is the 'spouse' of Israel, a powerful metaphor from marriage, but God does not kiss, does not fondle, does not caress or show any other bodily signs of affection for Israel. Again, according to Frymer-Kensky, because God is not a model for sexuality, in the rituals there is a strict separation between the sexual and the holy. The sexual is reserved for mortal human beings, and the emphasis on the difference between the sexes underlines the difference between God and human beings. Circumcision symbolically inscribes on the male body its own incompleteness and vulnerability, whereas the *nidda* laws, which relate to female blood, emphasize the special nature of the feminine. The word *nidda* comes from *nadad*, which means something like 'removed', 'separated'.[15] The *nidda* laws are often translated as regulations for cleanness and interpreted as a devaluation of the female body during menstruation and after childbirth. But it is nonsense to assume that in a religious tradition in which descendants and procreation are among the highest goods (and, at least in the Orthodox interpretation, no unmarried man is admitted to the rabbinate or to liturgical functions in the synagogue), the woman is given a negative role specifically at those moments when she has given life or her body shows symptoms of her capacity to conceive and bear a child. So in the case of *nidda* laws the function of the laws of cleanness seem to lie in the emphasis on sexual difference (which also sheds another light on the different lengths of continence after the birth of a son and the birth of a daughter), and this determines not only the life of the woman but also that of the man: the fact that a married man lives in the rhythm of separation from his wife and that the rabbis are most intimately familiar with the functions of the female body caused Susannah Heschel to ask: 'Whose vagina is it? Or is the vagina to be understood as a sign, perhaps parallel to the phallus, a sign which is loaded with that emotional significance which is formed by sexual identity . . . ? The *nidda* laws make the vagina a transcendent sign of the identity of the sexes and Jewish status.'[16]

Emphasis on the difference between the sexes on the one hand emphasizes the connection between sexuality and procreation: in fact in Hebrew the word for procreation is also used as a synonym for sexuality.[17] But conversely, the stress on the connection between sexuality and procreation also emphasizes the difference between the sexes: as the basis of desire and as a reference to human morality. More than one theorist has pointed out[18] that we can also read from the Talmud that the *nidda* laws which prohibit sexual intercourse at certain times also maintain structures of desire.[19] Here not only does sexuality appear as a 'necessary function' of procreation, but procreation also appears as a function of sexuality. If the incompleteness of human beings and the difference between human beings and God is emphasized by the difference between the sexes, procreation itself appears as a 'means' of continually reminding human beings of this incompleteness.

2. *Christianity: symbiosis of the sexes*

The Christian ordering of the sexes – and thus also of sexuality – is based on quite different premises from those of Judaism. In that the Christian God has assumed a human body in his Son, the difference between God and human beings is done away with. That is the real Christian message of salvation which is celebrated solemnly in the eucharist, the union of the divine and the human body. In becoming human and a body the Christian God also assumes a gender, or more precisely two genders. That is shown by many depictions from the Middle Ages and early modernity, which the mediaevalist Caroline Walker Bynum[20] and the art historian Leo Steinberg[21] have investigated. It is clear from the depictions which these scholars reproduce that unlike the God of Israel, the image of the redeemer in no way ceases below the waist and is sexually coded in two ways. From a series of depictions from the Middle Ages Bynum shows that the body of the saviour was endowed with all the signs of femininity: his sacrificial blood came to be shown as a female bosom providing nourishment. And in many depictions the wound even takes the form of a bleeding vulva – a depiction which also emerges in the texts of many female mystics. By contrast, Steinberg produces numerous depictions which emphasize the masculinity of the redeemer. Not only does the mother of God point to the member of the newborn saviour; the genitals are also emphasized time and again in depictions of the crucified and dead Christ, so that Steinberg makes a connection between erection and resurrection. According to Steinberg this erection means overcoming the flesh.[22] This twofold sexual coding of the body of the redeemer led on the one hand to the strong sexualization of religion, as expressed, for example, in the sermons and treatises of Meister Eckhart – and also by Abelard, Bernard of Clairvaux or other mystics. On the other hand the ideal of an erotic union with God influenced the symbolic ordering of the sexes and sexuality itself – in a way comparable to what happened in Judaism, but the other way round.

Whereas in Judaism the difference between God and human beings is also emphasized with a stress on the difference between the sexes, the Christian ideal of a union with God leads to the ideal of a symbiosis of the sexes. Therefore Paul's metaphors for marriage also resemble his images of the eucharist. 'Because there is one bread,' he said, 'we many are one body' (I Cor. 10.17). He calls individual believers 'members' who form an indivisible body with Christ (Rom. 12.5; see also I Cor. 12.12, 27). Christ is the head of the community and this is his 'body' (Eph. 5.23, 38); likewise in marriage, too, the man is to be the head of the woman and she is to form his body. And Paul goes even further: 'So too husbands, love your wives as your own body. Whoever loves his wife loves himself' (Eph. 5.28). The doctrine of the indissolubility of marriage which Christianity is the only religion of the world to have proclaimed cannot be expressed more clearly than in the image of a head which marries its own body.

This metaphor of marriage was later also to stamp secular conceptions – as when the king 'marries' the nation at his coronation:[23] one of many examples of the way in which the collective body reflects the individual sexual body along with cultural coding. The Christian idea also continues at the level of individual sexuality. That has been demonstrated, for example, by Peter Gardella in his book *Innocent Ecstasy: How Christianity gave America an Ethic of Sexual Pleasure*, in which he shows how the Christian doctrine of the 'innocent ecstasy' of the mystics helped to prepare the way for the sexual emancipation of the twentieth century.[24] One of the champions of this movement was Margaret Sanger, who – as a believing Christian – founded the American Movement for Birth Control. In her book *Happiness in Marriage* she expressed the view that sexual satisfaction, incarnated in simultaneous orgasms, was to be regarded as a sacrament. Birth control was necessary to give couples the possibility of perfecting their sexual technique in such a way that at the moment of orgasm they 'can attain the spiritual mystery of a communion of the two natures'.[25] For her, the symbiotic ordering of the sexes and the dogma of the indissolubility of marriage had become the synchronous act of sex.

Translated by John Bowden

Notes

1. I have investigated the significance of the framework of the media for the formation of communities in Christina von Braun, *Versuch über den Schwindel. Religion, Schrift, Bild, Geschlecht*, Zurich and Munich 2001.
2. Sigmund Freud, *Moses and Monotheism*, in *Complete Works* 23, London 1964, p.114.
3. Ibid., p.113.
4. *Theologische Realenzyklopäadie* VI, p.526.
5. Ibid., p.501.
6. I Cor. 11.7.
7. Gen. 1.27.
8. Augustine, *De Trinitate*, XII, 10.
9. Cf. Karin Elisabeth Borresen, *Subordination and Equivalence*, Washington, DC nd (c. 1981), pp.25–30; for the further development of this notion in Thomas Aquinas see Joseph Francis Hattel, *FEMINA UT IMAGO DEI in the Integral Feminism of St Thomas Aquinas*, Rome 1993, pp.280–4.
10. Meister Eckhart, *Deutsche Predigten und Traktate*, edited with a German translation by Josef Quint, Zurich 1979, p.399.
11. Id., 'Reden der Unterweisung', in ibid., pp.83f.
12. Meister Eckhart, 'Betrachtungen, Trostschrift', in *Schriften*, translated by Hermann Büttner, Düsseldorf 1959, p.271.
13. David Biale, *Eros and the Jews. From Biblical Israel to Contemporary America*, New York 1992, p.217.
14. Tykwa Frymer-Kensky, 'Law and Philosophy: The Case of Sex in the Bible', in Jonathan Magonet (ed.), *Jewish Explorations of Sexuality*, Providence and Oxford 1995, pp. 3–16: 4.
15. Hannah Rockman, 'Sexual Behaviour among Ultra-Orthodox Jews: A Review of Laws and Guidelines', in ibid.
16. Susannah Heschel, 'Sind Juden Männer? Können Frauen jüdisch sein? Die gesellschaftliche Definition des männlichen/weiblichen Körpers', in Sander L. Gilman, Robert Jütte and Gabriele Kohlbauer-Fritz (eds), *Der 'schejne Jidd'. Das Bild des 'jüdischen Körpers' in Mythos und Ritual*, Vienna 1998, pp.86–96: 95.
17. Daniel Boyarin, 'Dialectics of desire: "The evil instinct is very good"', in Magonet, *Jewish Explorations of Sexuality* (n.14), p.33.
18. Biale, *Eros and the Jews* (n.13), pp.212f.
19. Talmud: b. Niddah 31b.
20. Caroline Walker Bynum, *Fragmentation and Redemption. Essays on Gender and the Human Body*, New York 1991.
21. Leo Steinberg, *The Sexuality of Christ in Renaissance Art and Modern Oblivion*, New York 1983, second enlarged edition Chicago and London 1996.
22. Steinberg refers to Renaissance depictions, including those by Andrea Mantegna, Maerten van Heemskerck etc., see ibid., plates 45, 91–6.

23. Ernst H. Kantorowicz, *Die zwei Körper des Königs. Eine Studie zur politischen Theologie des Mittelalters*, translated by Walther Theimer and Brigitte Helimann, Munich 1990.
24. Peter Gardella, *Innocent Ecstasy: How Christianity gave America an Ethic of Sexual Pleasure*, New York and Oxford 1985.
25. Margaret Sanger, *Happiness in Marriage*, New York 1939, p.141.

II. Theological and Historical Reflections

Re-evaluating the Body in Eco-feminism

ROSEMARY RADFORD RUETHER

I. Formless matter (from *Enuma Elish* to Plato)

The Babylonian creation story, the *Enuma Elish*, was shaped in its final form from earlier materials by Babylonian priests about 1800 BC. Its story is revelatory of the relation between the male ruling class, women and nature that was emerging in early urban civilization in the ancient Near East and which has shaped Western civilization to the present. In this story we glimpse a change of consciousness from one of dependency on natural processes of generation to one in which dominant humans turn living nature into 'dead matter' and shape it according to the constructs of their mind. War, killing and the artisan craft are the metaphors for the construction of nature through human power and intellect.

The first half of the *Enuma Elish* reflects a theogony modelled on natural gestation. Starting with the primal pair of Mummu-Tiamat and Apsu, the generations of gods and goddesses are begotten and gestated. But a conflict breaks out between the older and younger generations of the gods. Having killed their primordial father, the younger gods face the wrath of the primal mother, Tiamat. They appoint Marduk as their champion who meets Tiamat in hand-to-hand combat. Marduk drives an arrow into her body and kills her. Standing on her body (the stance of a victor towards a vanquished enemy) he viewed her body that he might 'do artful works'. Marduk then split the body of the primal Mother, now reduced to dead matter. One side he lifted up to fashion the sky and its planetary lights; the other half becomes the earth below. Tiamat's consort Kingu was then seized and sacrificed, mingling his blood with clay to fashion human beings, making them the slaves of the gods, so the gods could be freed of labour.[1]

This story enshrines a relation of gods to humans as analogous to the relation of a leisure class to slaves who do the work that supports the rulers. The story also mirrors the new relation of this dominant class to nature as one based on war and death. Through killing, living beings following their own way of life are turned into 'raw materials' or 'resources' for human artisan construction.[2]

In the Hebrew creation story (Genesis 1) this transformation is already presupposed. God as transcendent (male) agent 'speaks' and the formless abyss is transformed into the heavens and the earth. In Plato's *Timaeus*, the Greek philosophical creation story, the death of the primal Mother, her transformation into inert matter, is also presupposed. For Plato there are two primal realities out of which the third, the visible creation and human beings, were shaped. The first is eternal Mind enshrining the intellectual forms or prototypes of all things that are to be generated. The other is a formless 'receptacle' which Plato calls the 'nurse' or 'space'. It has absolutely no form of its own and hence is unintelligible, but thereby is susceptible to receive all forms imprinted upon it.[3]

The Creator or 'Artisan' is the active agent that impresses the eternal forms on this passive 'receptacle' and thus shapes them into the primal elements of air, water, fire and earth and from these into the cosmos. The eternal Ideas and its agent the Artisan are likened to the Father, while the formless receptacle is the Mother. All being, agency, form and intelligibility come from the transcendent realm of Mind. 'Matter' or body is derived from that formless, unintelligible 'space' that receives the forms imprinted upon it, but also resists formation and thus is the principle of imperfection, sensibility and finitude.

The human soul, itself a particle of the world soul shaped by the Creator to make the Cosmos a living being, belongs ultimately to the heavenly world. To return to its true home, it must resist the passions that arise from the body and live a life of 'mortification' culminating in the separation of the soul from its inferior vehicle of the body in order to return to its 'native star'. If it fails to do this, it will be reincarnated into a lower form of life, 'such as a woman or an animal'.[4] Here a hierarchy of male over female, human over animal is assumed, mirroring the hierarchy of soul over body. Our true home is not in the body on earth, but in a heavenly disembodied state.

II. Transformation into eternal life (classical Christianity)

The hierarchy of heaven over earth, mind or soul over body, as male over female, deeply shaped classical Christianity as it moved out of the Hebrew into the Graeco-Roman world from the first to the fifth centuries AD. But Christianity was also shaped by a contrary idea unintelligible in terms of these Greek dualisms, the belief in the resurrection of the body. As Peter Brown has shown in his classic study, *The Body and Society*,[5] this gave Christian asceticism a much more radical goal than that found in Greek philosophy, content merely to control the body while still giving it its due. Christian ascetics focussed much more insistently on the body, and the repression of its needs for food, sleep and sexual urges, because they had more profound vision of its potential for transformation.

The body, rather than being doffed at death to allow the soul to soar alone into immortal life, was expected by the Christian to be transformed into what St Paul called 'the spiritual body' (I Cor. 15. 42–4), losing its urges for food, sex and sleep that expressed its fall into mortality. This spiritual body, purged of its fallen mortal expressions, would join the soul in a transformed cosmos of eternal life. The ascetic rigours themselves express the beginnings of this purgation of the body to recover its original spiritual nature.

Gregory of Nyssa imagines this process of the transformation of the body as like doffing a ragged tunic. This analogy is rooted in the Greek patristic exegesis of Genesis 3.7 in which Adam and Eve's putting on 'coats of skin' after the Fall is interpreted as a fall from an immortal into a mortal body.

> So we too, when we have cast off that dead, unsightly tunic, made from the skins of brutes and put upon us (for I take the 'coats of skins' to mean that conformation belonging to a brute nature with which we were clothed when we became familiar with passionate indulgence) shall, along with the casting off of that tunic, fling from us all the belongings that were around us of that skin of a brute: and such accretions are sexual intercourse, conception, parturition, impurities, suckling, feeding, evacuation, gradual growth to full size, prime of life, old age, disease and death . . . The Divine power, in the superabundance of Omnipotence, does not only restore you that body once dissolved, but makes great and splendid additions to it . . . the human being deposits in death all those peculiar surroundings which it has acquired from passionate propensities: dishonour, I mean, and corruption and weakness and characteristics of age; and yet the human being does not lose itself. It changes . . . into incorruption, that is, glory, and honour and power and absolute perfection; into a

condition in which its life is no longer carried on in the ways peculiar to mere nature, but has passed into a spiritual and passionless existence.[6]

This view of the body as capable of transformation into eternal life as the companion of the immortal soul presupposes a different view of body from that of Plato. Rather than being a formless 'receptacle' that enshrined the principle of finitude and spacio-temporal existence, body here suggests an ontological substratum of being that is a created expression of and upheld by divine being itself. This was the original spiritual body of the first creation, distorted into finitude through the fall but capable of purging these finite expressions through ascetic rigors that themselves anticipate that final transformation of the resurrected body.

As Caroline Bynum has shown in her important article on the body in mediaeval mysticism,[7] the spirituality of mystics, particularly women mystics, assumed a consubstantiality between the incarnate, crucified and resurrected body of Christ and that of the mystic. As the 'female' side of the soul-body relation, the body of Christ is particularly related to the body of the woman mystic who experienced in her own sufferings the transformative process already anticipated in Christ's resurrected body, a process that will turn the body into a vehicle of the immortal soul at the resurrection.

Bynum rightly protests against some modern feminist critique of Christianity that the mediaeval Christian view of the body-soul relation cannot be seen as mere footnotes to Plato. A new element that values the body as a vehicle of the soul's transformation into immortal life has changed the body-soul relation in Christianity. Yet it must also be clear from the above that it is not the finite body, the mortal flesh of earth, that Christianity valued, but its potential for being purged of all such finite limits, while still retaining an ontological substratum of the created person that can accompany the soul when the finite life of earth itself is transformed into eternal life. The mediaeval world valued the bodily, the sacramentality of water, bread, earth, and the virginal and martyred bodies of saints, but only as manifestations and pointers to a transformed body freed of mortal 'dross', not body in its 'natural' or, to Christian eyes, 'fallen' form.

III. Shifts in modern time

1. Only the disembodied word (Reformation)

The Renaissance, Reformation and birth of early modern science represents a series of shifts in this mediaeval vision, at once reclaiming of the world of nature as the human sphere of power and control and the loss of the vision of the sacramental body. The Calvinist and Reformed tradition particularly dismembered the mediaeval sense of the sacramentality of nature. For Calvinism 'nature' was 'totally depraved'. There was no residue of a divine presence in bodily nature that could sustain a natural knowledge of and relation to God. Saving knowledge of God came from above, transcendent to the bodily, visible world as the revealed word available only through scripture.

Populist Calvinism was notable for its iconoclastic hostility to visual representations of the sacred. Stained glass, statues and carvings were smashed and the churches stripped of all visible imagery. At the same time Reformed Christians must be purged of their attachment to 'sacramentals', holy water, blessed palms, relics of saintly flesh and bones, physical tokens of the sacred that could be contacted through touch.[8]

Nothing 'natural' could be bearers of the sacred. Only the disembodied word, read from biblical revelation, expounded through the preached word, could be bearers of the divine presence, but not in a form that humans can touch, smell, eat or hold. Even the sacrament of the eucharist was looked at with suspicion in its physicality and reinterpreted as an intellectual reminder of the saving act of Christ in the past, rather than its embodied presence today.[9] While Calvinism dismantled the sacramental world of mediaeval Christianity, it maintained and reinforced its demonic universe.

The fallen world, physical nature, and especially human groups outside the control of the Reformed church, lay in the grip of the Devil. All that was labelled 'pagan', whether unconverted Africans or Indians, or unreformed Catholics, were the playground of demonic powers. (Catholics returned the complement towards Protestants whom they saw as 'heretics'.) For both Protestants and Catholics, women continued to be the prime 'gateway' for the entrance of the demonic into society, their feeble minds and passions easily prey to the Devil, if not strictly controlled by fathers and husbands, ministers and magistrates.[10]

2. Nature as icon of divine reason (modern science)

The revolution of early modern science at first moved in a different direction, exorcising the demonic powers from nature in order to reclaim it as an icon of divine reason manifest in natural law, knowable to the reason of the scientist. But in the seventeenth century the more animist traditions of the 'nature magicians', such as Paracelsus, lost out to a strict dualism of transcendent intellect and dead matter. Nature was secularized. It no longer was the scene of a struggle between Christ against the devil, sacramental versus demonic embodiment. Both divine and demonic spirits were driven out of bodily nature. In Cartesian dualism and Newtonian physics bodily nature becomes matter in motion, dead particles (atoms) pushed or pulled by material force, moving obediently according to laws knowable to the new male priesthood of scientists.

The mediaeval world was suspicious of these who sought control over nature for its own sake, imagining such powers to come from the Devil. Its spirituality endorsed poverty and simple living, which did not prevent luxury, but did not glory in wealth as an expression of divine favour. Proponents of the scientific method, such as Francis Bacon, however, saw in it a new gospel of redemption. The Fall of 'man' was seen as a loss of control over nature, while the technological application of scientific reason promised to overcome this fall through restoring 'man's' control over nature. In a metaphor for scientific investigation borrowed from the torture chamber of witch hunters, Bacon exhorted the scientist to 'vex' nature and 'force her to yield her secrets'.[11] Again 'nature' is imagined as a female being whose dangerous autonomy must be defeated to subjugate 'her' to control. As in the Tiamat myth of ancient Babylon, the living Mother, once turned into 'dead matter', could be infinitely reconstructed as a source of power and wealth.

This process of control over nature through the technological application of scientific knowledge began to yield great profits in the industrial revolution of the eighteenth and nineteenth centuries. But this increasing technological triumph of science was preceded in the sixteenth century by the opening of vast new sources of wealth, land and cheap labour through colonialism. From the sixteenth into the twentieth centuries Western Europeans would appropriate the lands of the Americas, Asia and Africa and reduce its human populations to servitude. The wealth accrued by this vast expropriation of land and labour, with its fruits in export crops, precious metals and minerals, would fund new levels of technological development, transforming material resources into new forms of energy and mechanical work, control of disease, increasing speed of travel and communication. Western élites grew increasingly optimistic, imagining that this technological way of life would gradually conquer all material scarcity and even push back the limits of human mortality. The Christian dream of immortal blessedness, freed from the finite limits of the body, was translated into scientific, technological terms.

IV. The nightmare of the progress

However, in a short three-quarters of a century this dream of infinite progress has begun to be turned into a nightmare. The medical conquest of disease, lessening infant mortality, doubling the span of life of the affluent, insufficiently matched by birth limitation, has created a population explosion that is rapidly outrunning food supply. The gap between rich and poor, between the wealthy of industrialized sectors and the impoverished masses, especially in the former colonized continents of Latin America, Asia and Africa, grows ever wider. At the same time the non-human world of air, water and soil has been stretched to the breaking point. Carbon dioxide and other wastes thrown off by burning fossil fuels threatens the ozone layer that protects life on earth from excessive radiation from the sun. Polluted lakes and oceans grow incapable of supporting marine life. The soil becomes salty from over-irrigation and is turned into deserts. A question mark is poised over the whole process of human increase in numbers and the expanding consumerism of élites at the expense of the rest of the earth and the majority of humans.

The warning bell on this process of expansion has been sounded since the Club of Rome report in the late 1960s.[12] But leaders of affluent nations, particularly the United States, refuse to hear the wake-up call, except in the most token expressions, while the poor nations protest against the demand that the health of the planet should be preserved by curbing their struggles to emerge from poverty. A sharply divergent set of roads appear to direct humans to different ways of imagining the future.

On the one hand, there is the siren song that insists that the ecological crisis can be solved with more science applied to new forms of technology. The communications revolution seems to promise the ultimate release from the body into a 'virtual reality' of electronic signals. Face-to-face relations in embodied communities is not necessary when one can have global 'chat rooms' through computers. Progress can still be infinite, freed from the limitations of finite matter.

A different path is charted by the ecological movement. Ecologists call for a profound reconstruction of the foundational relations of mind and body, male and female, human and nature, that has shaped Western industrial society for the last five hundred years, if not before, perhaps going back to its roots in the rise of patriarchal societies in early urban cultures of the ancient Near East of the fifth millennium BC.

Some 'ecologians', such as Thomas Berry and Brian Swimme,[13] look hopefully to post-Newtonian science with its recognition that the dualism of 'dead matter' and transcendent mind no longer governs our view of the universe. What we perceive as body is itself a dynamic manifestation of energy in motion, continually transforming and reconfiguring itself on the subatomic, atomic, organic and cosmic levels. Human beings are latecomers to the planet, not its predestined rulers. We need to embrace this whole process of earth and cosmic creativity as our own source and basis of life, rather than imagining that we can rule over it and/or flee from it into some transcendent world not subject to its limits.

Rethinking 'our' relation to body and nature also entails rethinking relations with those groups of people stereotyped as expressions of body rather than mind, women in relation to men, blacks and indigenous people in relation to Europeans, working class and poor in relation to ruling class. A new ethic of mutuality needs to govern our relations with each other as humans, as well as our relation to our own bodies and the embodied world of plants and animals, earth, air and soil that sustains our lives.

Conclusion

Can this call to reshape our relation to our own bodies, to embodied other humans we have inferiorized as indentured labour and finally to the earth itself, provide the key to a sustainable future, rescuing us from a false path taken by human civilization for millennia? It is hard to imagine such a profound transformation of both consciousness and embodied relations happening on a global scale in a system so deeply shaped by the power of the wealthy few over global resources. The beneficiaries of this system are deeply alienated from nature in our technological encasements, while the impoverished majority rattle our cages. It is all too easy to imagine a contrary future in which human folly finally snaps the carrying capacity of the earth and we are sloughed off as a parasitic species, like the ancient dinosaurs.

Perhaps the best we can do is to give up the dreams of total solutions that will deliver the whole earth and everyone on it into a 'new heaven and earth' and content ourselves with a myriad of local solutions, each of which seeks to learn to live in harmony with each other and with our bioregion. From this expanding plurality of local transformations in a global network of communication and mutual support perhaps we can gain momentary glimpses of harmony of mind and body, human and human, human and nature, in the midst of finite life. Thereby we might yet preserve a sustainable earth to be passed down to our children and our children's children.

Notes

1. See 'The Creation Epic', in *Religions of the Ancient Near East: Sumero-Akkadian Religious Texts and Ugaritic Epics* ed. Isaac Mendelsohn, New York: Liberal Arts Press 1955, pp. 17–46.
2. For discussion, see Rosemary Radford Ruether, *Gaia and God: An Ecofeminist Theology of Earth Healing*, San Francisco: Harper San Francisco and London: SCM Press 1992, pp. 16–19.
3. Plato, *Timaeus*, pp. 49–52; see *The Dialogues of Plato* ed. B. Jowett, Vol. 2, New York: Random House 1937, pp. 29–32. For a discussion of Plato's view of matter in post-modern linguistic philosophy, see Judith Butler, *Bodies that Matter: The Discursive Limits of Sex*, London: Routledge 1993, pp. 36–49.
4. Ibid, 42, p. 23; also 90–91, pp. 66–67.
5. Peter Brown, *The Body and Society: Men, Women and Sexual Renunciation in Early Christianity*, New York: Columbia University Press 1988.
6. Gregory Nyssa, 'On the Soul and the Resurrection', in *Nicene and Post-Nicene Fathers*, 2nd series, Vol. 5, New York: Parker 1893, pp. 464–5.
7. Carolyn Bynum, 'Why all the Fuss about the Body? A Medievalist's Perspective', *Critical Inquiry*, Autumn 1995 (vol. 22/1), pp. 1–33. See also Rosemary Radford Ruether, *Women and Redemption: A Theological History*, Minneapolis: Fortress Press 1998, pp. 97–104.
8. For a discussion of the repression of sacramentals in the Protestant Reformation, see particularly Susan Karant-Nunn, *The Reformation of Ritual: An Interpretation of Early Modern Germany*, London: Routledge 1997.
9. See Rosemary Radford Ruether, *Christianity and the Making of the Modern Family*, Boston: Beacon Press 2000, pp. 73–9.
10. Catholic views of women as witches are enshrined in the 1486 treatise by the Domincans Johann Sprenger and Heinrich Kramer, *Malleus Maleficarum*, trs Montague Summers, London: Pushkin Press 1948. For the counter-part Protestant view, see William Perkins, *A Discourse on the Damned Art of Witchcraft* (1596).
11. For the connections between the practice of witch hunting and early modern science, see Brian Easlea, *Witch Hunting, Magic and the New Philosophy*, New Jersey: Humanities Press 1980. Also see Carolyn Merchant, *The Death of Nature: Women, Ecology and the Scientific Revolution*, San Francisco: Harper San Francisco 1980, pp. 163–91.
12. *The Club of Rome Report* was originally published in 1968 and warned that the present system of global expansion of production and consumption on which the concept of economic 'progress' was based was unsustainable.
13. See Thomas Berry and Brian Swimme, *The Universe Story*, San Francisco: Harper San Francisco 1992.

The World as God's Body

SALLIE MCFAGUE

> Since I do indeed exist and yet would not exist unless you were in me, why do I ask you to come to me?... Therefore, my God, I would not exist at all, unless you were in me; or rather, I would not exist unless I were in you 'from whom and by whom and in whom all things exist'... To what place do I call to you to come, since I am in you? Or from what place are you to come to me? Where can I go beyond the bounds of heaven and earth, that my God may come to me, for he has said: 'I fill heaven and earth?'
>
> Augustine, *Confessions*, I.2

If God is always incarnate, then Christians should attend to the model of the world as God's body. For Christians, God did not become human on a whim; rather, it is God's nature to be embodied, to be the One in whom we live and move and have our being. In Christianity, the God-world relationship is understood in light of the incarnation; hence, creation is 'like' the incarnation. Jesus Christ is the lens, the model, through whom Christians interpret God, world, and themselves. The doctrine of creation for Christians, then, is not different in kind from the doctrine of the incarnation: in both God is the source of all existence, the One *in whom* we are born and re-born. In this view, the world is not just matter while God is spirit; rather, there is a continuity (though not an identity) between God and the world. The world is flesh of God's 'flesh'; the God who took our flesh in one person, Jesus of Nazareth, has always done so. God is incarnate, not secondarily but primarily. Therefore, an appropriate Christian model for understanding creation is the world as God's body. This is not a description of creation (there are no descriptions); neither is it necessarily the only model; it is, however, one model that is commensurate with the central Christian affirmation that God is with us in the flesh in Jesus Christ and it is a model that is particularly appropriate for interpreting the Christian doctrine of creation *in our time*. Its merits and limitations should be considered in relation to other major models of the God-world relationship: God as clockmaker winding up the machine, as king of the realm, as father with wayward children, as personal agent acting in the world, and so forth.

Introduction: an appropriate model

The world as God's body is appropriate for our time (as well as being in continuity with the Christian incarnational tradition) because it encourages us to focus on 'the neighborhood'. It understands the doctrine of creation not to be primarily about God's power, but about God's love: how we can live together, all of us, within and for God's body. It focusses attention on the near, on the neighbour, on the earth, on meeting God not later in heaven but here and now. We meet God in the world and especially in the flesh of the world: in feeding the hungry, healing the sick, liberating the oppressed. An incarnational understanding of creation says nothing is too lowly, too physical, too mean a labour if it helps some creature to flourish. We find God in caring for the garden, in loving the earth well.

The doctrine of creation in this view is a practical, not an intellectual affair. It is not about God's absolute power (hence, one need not be disturbed by the lack of *ex nihilo* in Genesis!). The point of the doctrine is not to elevate God while demeaning us and the world; rather, it is to focus attention on our home, our garden planet. In Genesis God not only tells Adam and Eve to care for the garden, but also how good it is: after each act of creation in Genesis 1 God 'saw that it was good'. After completing the entire creation, 'God saw everything that he had made, and indeed, it was very good' (Gen. 1.31a). Interestingly, God does not say that it is good for human beings or even good for me, God, but simply good. This is an aesthetic response expressing appreciation for the intrinsic value of each and every creature, plant, and planetary process (sun, moon, earth, water). As Irenaeus would suggest later: 'The glory of God is every creature fully alive.'

Hence, this understanding of creation asks us to find out about the neighbourhood so we can take care of it. It suggests that human beings are not the only creatures that matter; however, we are special. We are the caretakers, the ones who can help the garden flourish, help the body of God be well fed and healthy – or we can destroy it. We *know* the difference between good and evil: the unique feature of human beings as well as our greatest burden is that *we know that we know*. We not only know how to do many things (all animals know this), but we *know* that we can do many things, and that some of these things are good and some bad for God's creation, God's body, our planetary garden.

Let us look more carefully at three implications of this model of creation and providence, that is, of how God and the world are related and who cares for the world. The implications of the model of the world as God's body are, first, that we must know our world and where we fit into it; second, that we must acknowledge God as the only source of all life, love, truth, and goodness; and third, that we realize that while God is in charge of the world, so are we.

I. Knowing the body, tending the garden

In our model, the body of God is the entire universe; it is all matter in its myriad, fantastic, ancient and modern forms, from quarks to galaxies. More specifically, the body of God needing our attention is planet earth, a tiny piece of divine embodiment that is our home and garden. In order to care for this garden, we need to know about it; in order to help all creatures who constitute this body flourish, we need to understand how we humans fit into this body.

All understandings of creation rest on assumptions about what the world is like and where human belong in it. First century Mediterranean, mediaeval, and eighteenth-century views of the world and the place of humans differ; the twenty-first century view does as well. In our evolutionary, ecological view of reality, everything is interrelated and interdependent. 'Ecological unity' is both radically individualistic and radically relational. In an organism or body, the whole flourishes *only* when all the different parts function well; in fact, the 'whole' is nothing but each and every individual part doing its particular thing successfully. Nothing is more unified than a well-functioning body but, also, nothing relies more on complex, diverse individuality.

Hence, the neighbourhood that we have been set down in is one that we must learn to care for in all its diverse parts and needs. We must become 'ecologically literate', understanding its most basic law: that there is no way the whole can flourish unless *all parts* are cared for. This means distributive justice is the key to sustainability or, to phrase it differently, our garden home, the body of God, will only be healthy long term if *all* parts of it are cared for appropriately. Before all else, the community, our planet, must survive (sustainability) which it can do only if all members have access to basic necessities (distributive justice). We need to learn 'home economics', the basic rules of how our garden home can prosper – and what will destroy it. Most simply, these house rules are: Take only your share; clean up after yourself; and keep the house in good repair for others.

The World as God's Body

We must do so because, as the self-reflective part of God's body – the part that knows that we know – we have become partners with God in maintaining the health of creation. We are no longer the peak of creation, the one above all the others and for whom the others were made; rather, we are at one and the same time the neediest of all creatures and the most powerful. We cannot exist beyond a few minutes without air, a few days without water, or a few weeks without the plants but we are also, given our population and high-energy lifestyle, the one species that can undermine the planet's well-being, as global warming, the decline of biodiversity, and the increasing gap between the rich and the poor are illustrating. In a strange paradox, we who have unprecedented power over the planet are at the same time at its mercy: if it does not thrive, neither can we.

As is evident, this first implication of creation modelled as God's body supports and underscores a radically ecological view of the world. It is entirely opposed to the cult of individualism endorsed by modern religion, government, and economics, all of which claim that human beings are basically separate, isolated individuals who enter into relationships when they wish. This is the view of human beings that underlies both New Age and born-again Christianity, as well as market capitalism and American democracy ('life, liberty, and the pursuit of happiness'). Perhaps the most important implication of creation as God's body is the new anthropology it demands: we are – basically, intrinsically, and always – interrelational, interdependent beings who live in total dependence on the others who compose the body, while at the same time being responsible for the well-being of one tiny part of the body, planet earth.

II. God as source of life and love

A second implication of the model of creation as God's body is that it radicalizes both God's transcendence and God's immanence. This model has been criticized by some as pantheistic, as identifying God and the world. I do not believe it is. If God is to the universe as each of us is to our bodies, then God and the world are not identical. They are, however, intimate, close, and internally related in ways that can make Christianity uncomfortable, when it forgets its incarnationalism. But we Christians should not shy away from a model that radically underscores both divine transcendence and divine immanence. How does it do so?

In the world as God's body, God is the source, the centre, the spring, the spirit of all that lives and loves, all that is beautiful and true. When we say

'God', that is what we mean: we mean the power and source of all reality. *We are not the source of our own being; hence, we acknowledge the radical dependence of all that is on God.* This is true transcendence: being the source of everything that is. Our universe, the body of God, is the reflection of God's being, God's glory; it is the sacrament of God's presence with us. The most radically transcendent understanding of God is, then, at the same time the most radically immanent understanding. Because God is always incarnational, always embodied, we can see God's transcendence *immanentally*. Meeting God is not a momentary 'spiritual' affair; rather, God is the ether, the reality, the body, the garden *in which we live*. God is never absent; God is reality (being); everything that has being derives it from God (we are born of God and re-born by God). The entire cosmos is born of God, as is each and every creature. We depend on this source of life and renewable absolutely. We could not live a moment without the gifts of God's body–air, food, water, land, and other creatures. To realize this is an overwhelming experience of God's transcendence; it calls forth awe and immense gratitude. *Yet*, at the same time, as Augustine puts it, God is closer to us than we are to ourselves. Where can we go where God is not, since God fills heaven and earth: 'I would not exist if I were not in you.' The God whom we meet through the earth is not only the source of my being, but of all being. We see glimmers of God in creation (God's body) and we see the same God more clearly in Jesus Christ, the major model of God for Christians.

The second implication of our model, then, is that is allows us to meet God in the garden, on the earth, at home. We do not have to go elsewhere or wait until we die or even be 'religious'. We meet God in the nitty-gritty of our regular lives, for God is always present in every here and now. This second implication underscores the first: since God is here in our world, then surely it is indeed our neighbourhood, our planet and its creatures, that we should be caring for. *What other vocation could we have but to care for God's body?*

III. Who is in charge?

A third implication of our model of the world as God's body is that God alone is not in charge. Our model is not a mechanistic one: God does not control the world as a puppeteer controls puppets or a clockmaker starting a clock or a king commanding his subjects. Divine power is not unilateral – the more one party has, the less there is for the other. Rather, *God shares*: in organisms, power is mutual flourishing, empowerment, symbiosis; the whole does not flourish unless the parts are thriving. But this is a messy business and does not result in the well-being for all creatures all the time – how could it? If the body of God is billions of different species and individuals, each one with a desire to live, there will inevitably be many that do not survive or flourish. An evolutionary, ecological picture of reality is not neat, nice, or romantic. It is indifferent, often brutal, and sometime tragic. It is also often serendipitous: the same process that results in the AIDS virus or cancer cells created our brains and our emotions. Hence, so-called 'natural evil' will occur – frequently and for no reason, depending on one's perspective (a flood helps some creatures and devastates others). Add to natural evil what is called 'moral evil' or sin: the perversions of reality (of life, love, goodness, beauty, truth) which we human beings perpetrate, both individually and collectively, and one has an awesome task for providence.

A century that has known the holocaust, Hiroshima, and now global terrorism, not to mention ordinary poverty, discrimination and greed, does not need to be told how powerful evil is. But in our model of the world as God's body, even these monstrous examples of evil do not imply 'another' reality, an evil power, as it were. There is, in an incarnational creation story, only one reality: the world derives its being from God, lives within and towards God, and is 'real' to the extent it reflects the one reality, God. Evil does not 'exist'. It does not have ontological status; rather, it is a perversion of good. All that lives depends on God or comes from God; evil does not depend on God or come from God. This does not make it less powerful, less prevalent, or less tragic, but it does suggest that evil is not in charge, all appearances to the contrary. Christians believe that ultimately God is in charge: a doctrine of creation and providence without the resurrection would be a doctrine of despair. There is little in our world that suggests this; in fact, reading a daily newspaper is all one needs to refute it. It is 'absurd' to believe it. Perhaps believing in God may be nothing more than trusting that God *is* in charge – no matter what happens. H. Richard Niebuhr says that believing in Jesus Christ means becoming suspicious of one's 'own deep suspicion of the Determiner of Destiny'.[1]

We work this faith out here in our neighborhood. It is figuring out where we are even if we cannot know why we are here. If we see ourselves as within God's body, as tending the garden, as doing home economics for God's household, we can relax about some things and get busy with others. We can rest in the comfort of God's constant and enveloping presence, knowing that God holds the whole world in her hands. We can, at the same time, get busy learning about our neighbours and how we can all live here justly and sustainably.

We close with a reminder that all models are partial and inadequate. No *one* model is adequate, for each allows us to see some aspects of the God-world relationship, but shuts out others. The model of the world as God's body is meant as a corrective to the tradition, not as a substitute for it. It is offered as *one* model that is commensurate with Christianity's central incarnational belief and, for our time, helpful for the flourishing of all God's creatures. The final word, however, on this model and on all models is one of caution: 'Be careful how you interpret the world; it *is* like that.'[2]

Notes
1. H. Richard Niebuhr, *The Responsible Self*, New York: Harper and Row 1963, p. 175.
2. Erich Heller, *The Disinherited Mind*, World 1961, p. 211.

Dichotomy or Union of Soul and Body? The Origins of the Ambivalence of Christianity to the Body

JEAN-GUY NADEAU

The dichotomy between the body and the spirit which has come about in Christianity has often been denounced. But does such a dichotomy really exist in Christianity? Perhaps it does, if one understands by dichotomy a simple opposition between soul and body. However, the term dichotomy seems to me to be stronger than a designation of opposition; it suggests a radical division. Can we in fact speak of dichotomy in the strict sense when whatever happens to the body also happens to the soul? Can we use this term when sexual sin has been, and still is, largely held to be the worst of sins, and when divorcees who have remarried cannot receive communion in the Catholic Church unless 'they accept the commitment to live a life of total continence'?[1] Can we use it when half of humanity is still excluded from the ordained ministry in the Catholic Church on grounds of gender? Confronted with these facts we could even ask whether a dichotomy between soul and body could not have helped us to rid sexuality of the burden of guilt and the threat of hell. Finally, is not the imagery of hell and its torments the most evident testimony to the union that Christianity has always made between the soul and the body?

Based on the resurrection and the incarnation, the Christian tradition is perhaps the tradition which has attached most value to the body – created, raised, determinative for salvation and for relations with God. To recall a few examples: there are the Pauline exhortations to glorify God in our body (I Cor. 6.20; Phil. 1.20); to bear in our bodies the agony of Jesus and to manifest his life in them (II Cor. 4.10), to offer our bodies as a living sacrifice, holy and acceptable to God (Rom. 12.1). There is belief in the resurrection of the flesh; the conception of the sacraments as tangible signs and ways of grace and salvation; the transmission of original sin by a bodily liquid, though it also affects the soul; the imagery of hell (yes, again, but this example is so evocative); the role that the spiritual exercises of St Dominic and St Ignatius accord to the body in the call for and expression of spiritual experience; the dogma of the assumption of the Virgin Mary, 'who ascended to heaven with her soul and body'; the Sistine Chapel, which John Paul has described as 'a sanctuary of the theology of the human body',[2] and so on.

But where does this impression of dichotomy then come from? It has several sources. The one closest to us seems to me to be the fact that we read the texts of the tradition through the filter of Cartesian dualism, which promotes a disenchanted, mechanical and functional vision of the body, 'devoid of any spiritual essence or expressive dimension'.[3] Now this vision from which modernity has emerged is a thousand miles from the vision of the body and the deity put forward by the Gospels. On the one hand 'the word has been made flesh', in such a way that 'that which was from the beginning, which we have seen with our eyes, which we have looked upon and touched with our hands concerning the word of life – the life was made manifest ... we proclaim it to you' (I John 1.1–3). Moreover until recently a social and political control of the body was exercised openly throughout Christianity, whereas nowadays it is exercised in more subtle and more diffuse ways. So it is not surprising that calls for the liberation of the bodily subject are addressed to Christianity, all the more so since Christianity continues to stamp a number of political contexts.

Other sources of the opposition between the soul and the body are better known. This is a heritage of Greek metaphysics to which the tradition is not reduced; rather, it declares the Manichean version of such metaphysics to be a heresy, though it continues to be stamped by it. A quasi-sacralization of the Stoic ethic promoting the mastery of body by the spirit and the mortification of the flesh and the body was identified with passion, pleasure and sin. The vocation to asceticism and its temptation to escape the body was generalized and extended to all the faithful, thus perverting relations with the female body. All this meant that it proved possible to talk of a moral dichotomy between the body, which was bad, and the spirit, which was good. But it would be even more correct to speak of a subordination of the body to the soul, and more specifically to eternal salvation. If there has been mistrust of the body in Christianity, it is precisely because of the intimacy of its relation with the soul, the salvation of which it threatens. Hence the need to mortify the body, to purge it of passion, pleasure and sin. So here we have to talk of a dichotomy between salvation and pleasure, particularly sexual pleasure, and not of a dichotomy between soul and body. What follows, which is so brief that the necessary nuances cannot be introduced, aims to document to some degree this hypothesis of the intimate relation between the soul and the body in Christianity.

I. The gospel body

The incarnation affirms that the divine is written on human history in a quite particular, 'personal' way. With it the saving body and the saved body appear in 'the history of human beings, the story of God'. On the one hand the saving action of Jesus comes from his body: a body which is engaged in speaking as well as acting and touching, a body which is both fragile and powerful, a body which is both crucified and risen. On the other hand this action affects the body. Jesus saves, manifests and teaches salvation by significant gestures which relate to the body. Even today Christians have recourse to this saving power of Christ and file into various sanctuaries to touch a crucifix or a statue. To save is to manifest the presence of God by healing the heart and the spirit as well as the body – the Jewish tradition of Jesus and Paul had no need to list all these three. And if the historical person of Jesus is no longer present among us, the Christian faith affirms that we encounter it in others. Through service and care it is bodily action that proves to be the place of the encounter with God. Christians cannot separate love of God from care of neighbour. In the parable of the last judgment it is care for the body of the other which determines relations with God.

Finally, the body of Christ is also the eucharist, the body broken and shared. Although it causes problems today, the substantialist theology of the eucharist shows a concern to corporealize (or to materialize) the person of God himself, or at least the Son. If transubstantiation is so important in this theology, it is not only because the consecrated bread makes Christ present (a symbolic conception of this would be sufficient) but because by making it substance it increases its reality and allows the faithful to have a bodily relationship with him, to be *truly* (in other words bodily) close to him.

II. The saved body, a member of the Lord and a temple of the Spirit

Nevertheless it is from Paul that the theology of the Christian body is derived – a theological choice which is not an innocent one. This theology brings together in an original way elements from the Jewish tradition, Greek Stoicism and the Christian experience of the *ecclesia* (which I shall not be able to go into here). But it is difficult to speak of the body in Paul because his concept is so alien to our understanding, marked as it is by Cartesian dualism. It is also difficult, in that Paul uses the expression sometimes to denote the whole person, sometimes to denote the perishable body, and sometimes to denote the church of Christ. Be this as it may, in Paul the body is a major point of reference for denoting both tne disciple of Christ and his church. As Elisabeth Schüssler Fiorenza points out, 'Not the soul or mind or the innermost Self but the body is the image and model for our being church.'[4]

The Pauline theology of the body is primarily expressed in a key text (I Cor. 6.12–20) which was to determine the Christian view of the body both individually and collectively. According to this text, one who unites with a prostitute[5] forms a single body with her, even seizing the members of the Lord to make them members of the prostitute. This affirmation might seem excessive to the degree that it accords to sexual union, even with a prostitute, the same intensity as union with Christ. Such is the weight that Paul accords to the body and to sexual relations in the drama of salvation!

Confronted with an ethical and above all a communal problem, here the apostle was reacting to the Gnostic and dualistic anthropology of Christians in Corinth who thought that what affected the body should not affect the soul.[6] Now Paul's Jewish anthropology considers that a person is one with his or her body, to such a degree that the Lord who saves the person saves the whole person, including the body. As the object of the divine action, something that the Gnostics deny, the body is radically associated with the new life and the new being in Christ. This inevitably has consequences. How could Christians signify their redemption and the glory of the one who is in them, if not in their bodies? So those who have been redeemed could not act if they were still slaves, i.e. in the Stoic context, enslaved to their passions.

Stoic ethics is the second source of Paul's argument. I Corinthians has its setting in a world in which sexual intercourse, like food, is related to health and the necessary satisfaction of natural needs.[7] Now Stoic morality, which was concerned to free human beings from slavery to the passions, rejected this morality and aimed at submitting them to the control of reason, which is the specific attribute of the human being. Human nature is worthy, provided that its passions are controlled by reason; pleasure appears as a disturbance of the senses, as a result of which human beings lose their true nature.[8] Two Stoic maxims could even have directly influenced Paul's position on the body and prostitution or debauchery: 1. 'The man who has sexual relations with concubines sins against himself.' 2. 'A man pollutes the divinity in his being by any impure action.'[9] As Paul takes them over, they become: 1.

Dichotomy or Union of Soul and Body?

'Every other sin which a man commits is outside the body; but the immoral man sins against his own body.' 2. 'Do you not know that your body is a temple of the Holy Spirit within you, which you have from God?' (I Cor. 6.18–19).

Taking up this passage in I Corinthians, Augustine derived an exhortation and a conclusion from it which are particularly interesting in connection with his standpoints on prostitution[10] and the souls of women:.

> Brothers of Bulla ... You are the members of Christ ... Am I going to take the members of Christ to make them members of a prostitute? And our Christians not only give their heart to prostitutes, but involve in this stain women who were free from it – as if these creatures had no soul; as if the blood of Christ had not yet also been shed for them; as if scripture did not declare that prostitutes and tax-collectors will precede you into the kingdom of God.[11]

To return to Paul. Christianizing Stoic morality, he aims at respect and realization now for the saved body. Redeemed by the death of Christ, the Christian body is a member of Christ and a temple of the Holy Spirit. Hence the importance of its integrity, which is indissolubly physical and spiritual, the former in some way bearing witness to the latter. This is a theme which, as we know, the fathers will vie with one another in developing.

The last element in Paul's thought is that despite his desire to leave this body to regain the Lord, he affirms the resurrection of the body (I Cor. 15.42–4), i.e. of the whole person. But what is more significant for us, given the ambivalence of the term body in Paul, is the outcome that tradition and the creed have given to this affirmation, translating it 'resurrection of the flesh': *Credo in carnis resurrectionem*.

III. The body, the turning point between salvation ... and damnation

Stamped by Neoplatonism, the fathers moved away from Pauline anthropology and made a greater distinction between body and spirit than Paul did. As we know, several of them expressed a scorn for the body, but once again this was precisely because of its intimate connection with the soul: whatever affects, pollutes or purifies the body affects, pollutes or purifies the soul. For the fathers, bodily experience retains a crucial importance for determining salvation:

> The flesh is the turning point of salvation, in that whereas the soul is chosen by God for salvation, it is the flesh that makes it possible for the soul to be thus the choice of God. Thus the flesh is washed so that the soul is purified; the flesh receives unction so that the soul is consecrated; the flesh is marked with a sign so that the soul is protected; the flesh is covered with the shade of the imposition of hands so that the soul is illuminated by the spirit; the flesh feeds on the body and blood of Christ so that the soul may feed on the strength of God. So we cannot separate them in recompense, since they are united in service. For the flesh offers even sacrifices well-pleasing to God . . . to its own detriment.[12]

Here we are a long way from the gospel, according to which it is not that which goes into a man which makes him pure or impure. And we are all the further from the gospel, all the more so in that, as the turning point for salvation, the body is also the turning point for damnation. In other words, salvation and damnation pass through it. Along with the flesh and the passions, the body became suspect and an object of control, a control which was all the more necessary since eternal life was at stake. 'When one wants to seize a city,' a desert monk proclaimed, 'one cuts off water and provisions; it is the same with the passions of the flesh.'[13] In that case virginity appeared to be the best way of cutting of the passions, and of protecting the body and soul of Christian men, and particularly Christian women. 'No vase of gold or silver is as dear to God as the temple of a virgin body.'[14] Therefore, 'for women as for men, salvation depends above all on the chastity that we show. We are the temple of God in which the Holy Spirit has consecrated its dwelling, and chastity is the guardian and priestess of this temple.'[15]

The theme of pollution, inherited from the Hebrew world but contrary to the teaching of Jesus of Nazareth mentioned above, became established in budding Christianity. The ecclesiology of the body of Christ was fed by it, and already in Paul this led to the exclusion of those whose members might have polluted the whole body: 'If anyone is a brothel keeper he must cease or be excluded from the community. But a prostitute, a sodomite or someone who does that of which one cannot speak must be excluded from the community because he is polluted,' decreed Hippolytus of Rome. Mary Douglas already noted that Christian thought on the body was developed at a time when the Christian body was persecuted, and its physical and social integrity were contested. She saw here social conditions which readily leant themselves to beliefs that symbolized the body as an imperfect container which could be made perfect only by becoming impermeable.[16] Thus purity and virginity, its demonstrable corollary, became the qualifications *par excellence* of the body, and so it was that the body celebrated by the Assumption is a body exempt from any stain. With its emphasis on chastity and virginity, Christianity added to the Jewish theme of pollution, indeed disfigured it.

For the fathers, the bodily chastity of Christian men, and above all of Christian women, was such a radical value 'that for us the loss of chastity is more fearful than the penalty of the cruellest death'.[17] And John Chrysostom praised the young Pelagia who, 'on the advice and with the aid of Jesus Christ', preferred to deliver herself to death by throwing herself from the roof of her home than being stripped and perhaps raped by the soldiers who came to arrest her:

> Pains, torture, fearful punishment, she was ready to endure it all, but she feared losing the crown of virginity ... So she refused to appear before the court, to expose herself as a spectacle to licentious gaze, to allow impure desires to take delight in her features; she protected her sacred body from outrage; from the virginal chamber she passed to another haven of chastity, to heaven.[18]

So bodily experience in particular determines Christian identity. This is again witnessed by the typology of the prostitute, virgin or mother which defines her by her body and by the masculine appropriation of it. But theology treated and even demonized women's body above all as a threat. Theology has largely been the work of ascetics and hermits fleeing the world 'for whom the woman symbolizes what they have renounced and what constantly threatens their attachment to God'.[19] As the daughter of Eve associated with the passions, sex and the devil, the receptacle of the debauchery – though this is masculine – by which she communicates original sin, the woman is the other from whom one must protect oneself. And if she too must be protected, and against herself, this will most often be by imprisoning her.[20] Here again it is because of its dangerous proximity to the soul that the body – particularly the feminine body – is curbed, imprisoned and despised.

IV. The crucified body

I cannot conclude this brief survey without recalling the weight of the suffering of Jesus in the theology of redemption and the omnipresence of the crucified body in Christian, particularly Catholic, iconography. For example, many people will recall the images of the Sacred Face, of Christ crowned with thorns, or Christ by the column, bleeding from the marks of the scourge, which adorned many churches in our childhood. We cannot pass over in silence the importance attached to tradition by participation in the redemptive suffering of Christ, though we are aware of the repressive use to which this was put.[21] Certainly these sufferings, both those of Jesus and of the faithful, are not only bodily, but we cannot deny that the bodily sufferings have counted and still count for a great deal.

If part of theological discourse has tried to dissociate soul and body, this has not really proved successful; rather, light has been shed on their close connection. In fact the Christian tradition clearly states that what affects the one affects the other. If there is mistrust and even contempt for the body in Christianity, it is because the fate of the soul seems to be wholly determined by that of the body, whose promiscuity is seen as a threat. Conversely, however, in sharing and the sacraments, this promiscuity has proved to be salutary, and thus has always been a determinative factor.

Translated by John Bowden

Notes

1. John Paul II, speech at the conclusion of the Roman synod on marriage and the family, 25 October 1980.
2. Id., homily on the occasion of the reopening of the Sistine Chapel, 8 April 1994.
3. Charles Taylor, *Sources of the Self*, Cambridge, Mass. 1990, p. 145.
4. Elisabeth Schüssler Fiorenza, *In Memory of Her*, New York and London 1983, p. 380.
5. Here I use the traditional translation 'prostitute' for the Greek word *porne*, though one can doubt whether it is correct. Its use by the tradition is more important here than the accuracy of the translation.
6. J. Murphy O'Connor, 'Corinthian Slogans in 1 Co 6.12–20', *Catholic Biblical Quarterly* 40, 1978, p. 394. Cf. also Wayne A. Meeks, *The First Urban Christians*, New Haven 1983, p. 122.
7. G. Kittel (ed.), *Theological Dictionary of the New Testament* 6, Grand Rapids 1968, p. 582; John L. McKenzie, *Dictionary of the Bible*, Milwaukee 1965, p. 701.
8. This position was to mark the whole Christian tradition. Even Thomas Aquinas, who recognized it as intrinsically good, since it comes from God, considered that pleasure hinders a person from being entirely in the service of God, all the more so since there is a certain dirtiness in the discharge of semen, Mark Toon, *The Philosophy of Sex According to St Thomas Aquinas*, Washington 1954.
9. Kittel, *Dictionary* (n.7), p. 583.
10. Jean-Guy Nadeau, *La prostitution, une affaire de sens. Étude de pratiques socials et pastorals*, Montreal 1987.

11. Augustine, *Sermones* XVII, 7.
12. Tertullian, *The Resurrection of the Flesh*, VIII, PL 2, p. 806.
13. Quoted in Marcel Bernos et al., *Le fruit défendu*, Paris 1985, p. 66.
14. Jerome, quoted in France Quéré Jaulines, *La femme. Les grands texts des Pères de l'Église*, Paris 1968, p. 104.
15. Tertullian, quoted ibid, p. 142. See also the text from John Chrysostom quoted ibid, p. 182.
16. Mary Douglas, *Purity and Danger*, London 1966, p. 158.
17. Tertullian, *Apologeticum* L 12, Paris 1929, p. 108.
18. John Chrysostom, *Homilies on St Pelagius*, First Homily.
19. Eric Fuchs, *Le désir de la tendresse*, Geneva 1979, p. 110. Cf. also Michel Legrain, *Le corps humain, Du soupçon à l'évangélisation*, Paris 1978, p. 189.
20. Cf. Nadeau, *La prostitution* (n.10), pp. 251–76; id., 'Inculturation of Ecclesiology and Morals through Pastoral Ministry towards Prostitutes', *Catholic Theological Society of America Proceedings* 45, Louisville, Ky 1990, pp. 92ff.
21. Cf. Joanne C. Brown and Carole R. Bohn (eds), *Christianity, Patriarchy and Abuse. A Feminist Critique*, New York 1989.

Corporeality and Mysticism

TINA BEATTIE

Introduction: The writings of Catherine of Siena

I have recently returned from a holiday in Zambia where I had the opportunity to visit an AIDS hospice and orphanage, run by Catholic sisters. Since then, I have found myself reflecting on some of the challenges facing theology, as it seeks to embody itself in the many lives and contexts that make up the Christian community. There is an unacknowledged schism in 'body theologies' today, depending on whether they originate from theologians working in close contact with poor communities, or from Western academics working in more privileged cultural contexts. At the risk of over-generalization, I would suggest that Third World liberation theologians still focus on the crucified and suffering body as the privileged locus of theological revelation, while Western postmodernists and feminists tend to concentrate more on the gendered and sexual body. I do not think these perspectives are mutually exclusive, but it suggests the extent to which theology still faces the complex and multi-facetted task of integrating the multiple visions and voices that have emerged in recent years, within a coherent theological and ethical vision. This requires recognizing the ongoing reality that most bodies in our world are not well-fed Western bodies with access to clean water, food, health care and adequate housing, whose primary concerns are to achieve psychological, sexual and spiritual well-being. They are poor, neglected and sick bodies, that cry out for justice to a world deafened by power, militarism and wealth.

Related to this quest for a theology of the body that communicates the challenge as well as the promise of the Christian story, is a growing recognition that the appeal to experience which informs much modern theology, particularly feminist theology, is not in itself a sufficient basis for theological reflection.[1] There is a need to incorporate experiential perspectives within a shared Christian narrative that ultimately allows us to transcend our differences of time and place, to participate in the drama of the incarnation that is being played out between us and among us in the making of the world.

This means recognizing that experience only acquires meaning when it is interpreted according to shared linguistic, cultural or religious values, and therefore the experiencing body is primarily a discursive body when it becomes the locus of theoretical or theological reflection. Meaning and memory are vested not in the body itself, but in the language we use to interpret our bodily experiences, and therefore the quest for contextuality and corporeality in theological discourse is as much a question of style as of substance.

After the excessive emphasis on scientific approaches to knowledge that developed in the post-Enlightenment era and particularly in the nineteenth and early twentieth century, theology is rediscovering itself as literature, poetry and prayer. This suggests the possibility of a fruitful encounter between academic theology and the Christian mystical tradition. I want to focus on the mystical writings of Catherine of Siena (1347–80), with this suggestion in mind. Catherine belonged to a group of women affiliated with the Order of Saint Dominic, who committed themselves to the care of the poor and the sick in plague-ravaged Siena. She had a wide following and exerted considerable influence over Church politics. (She was instrumental in persuading Pope Gregory XI to return to Rome from exile in Avignon.)

Catherine's *Dialogue* is a form of mystical theology that expresses plurivocity, corporeality and desire in critical engagement with the doctrines and institutions of the church, while being committed to social justice and expressing solidarity with the poor and the marginalized. Notwithstanding her extreme practices of asceticism and self-starvation, she can be a source of inspiration for modern theologians looking to reconcile the particular and the universal, through forms of expression that allow the bodies of individual Christians and communities to speak from their particular contexts within the universal body of Christ and the Church. In Catherine's case, this gives rise to at least three different but inter-related 'bodies' – the mortal body, the transcendent body of the soul, and the sacramental body of Christ in the church and the eucharist.

I. Mystical theology

Religious studies scholars have tended to treat mysticism as a generic category of psychological experience that transcends religious and cultural differences, but several Christian theologians have challenged this theory.[2] Today there is a recognition that mysticism too is a contextual form of knowledge, arising not out of any direct unmediated experience of God or state of altered consciousness, but representing the quest of the believer to enter more fully – and therefore bodily – into the mystery of God through the doctrines, symbols and practices of his or her religious tradition. To quote Edith Wyschogrod: 'The saint does not experience body-as-such, but a time-bound, socially and historically conditioned saintly body.'[3]

In addition, there is a growing body of scholarship that considers the ways in which mystical texts bear the marks of sexual difference. Christianity with its Greek philosophical inheritance has tended to identify femininity with matter and emotion and masculinity with the spirit and reason, and this has shaped the language and practices of Christian spirituality. Scholars such as Caroline Walker Bynum and Grace Jantzen have drawn attention to the fact that bodily images and associations with food, including the eucharist, tend to feature more prominently in the writings of mediaeval women mystics than in those of men, and this was often accompanied by ascetic practices that today would be seen as symptomatic of anorexia nervosa or bulimia.[4] Jantzen argues that the tendency to treat the writings of women mystics as resources for private spirituality while ignoring the social context in which these were produced betrays the demands of social justice. She writes that in mediaeval Europe, women's holiness 'was bought at a price which no man would ever be expected to pay: acceptance of the gender stereotypes which made the identification of women with food, the flesh, and suffering service seem natural'.[5]

These are legitimate criticisms that are of particular relevance for those studying the life of Catherine of Siena. However, my concern is not with the pathological or psychological dimensions of Catherine's mysticism, significant though these are, but with her theological style. Bynum suggests that the complex relationship between food, the eucharist and the body in accounts of mediaeval female spirituality cannot be understood simply in pathological terms. She writes:

> The point of even the oddest of these stories was ultimately not rejection of the physical and bodily, but a finding of the truly physical, the truly nourishing, the truly fleshly, in the humanity of Christ, chewed and swallowed in the eucharist. Even here, physicality was not so much rooted out or suppressed as embraced and redeemed at that point where it intersected with the divine. So, in addition to the psychological and social explanations . . . there are theological and religious reasons for women's spirituality.[6]

It is these theological and religious reasons that concern me here, with a particular focus on the ways in which mystical texts are literary constructs in which the body symbolizes a range of meanings depending on its theological context.

What follows is a selective and partial reading that does not claim to offer a comprehensive survey of Catherine's theology. The *Dialogue* is not constructed as a linear argument but as a meditation that circles repetitively around key themes – self-knowledge, love and suffering; the relationship between the soul, the body and God; the eucharistic body of Christ; the Trinity; the mystical, maternal body of the church and the corruption of her priests and servants, and the universality of God's providence. It is an elaborate theological construct, dictated and edited by Catherine towards the end of her life, which brings together themes and reflections from her prolific correspondence addressed to a range of people including family, friends, clerics, popes and spiritual advisers. She presents her considerable theological wisdom in the form of a personalized exchange motivated not by intellectual curiosity but by love and longing for intimate union with God. The difference between her style and that of more systematic theology is that it is a discourse of invitation rather than persuasion, of desire rather than logic. We are invited to share her God, not because we are intellectually persuaded by her arguments, but because we have become infected with her desire.

Catherine's language is flamboyant and her imagery lush. She evokes the mystical union with the body of Christ in terms of lavish eucharistic imagery of embodiment and blood that are alien and maybe even repellant to some modern readers. In seminars I have sometimes used her famous letter describing how she accompanied a condemned man to the scaffold,[7] in conjunction with the feminist psycholinguistics of Luce Irigaray.[8] While students have shown a willingness to enter into the spirit of Irigaray's highly stylized and abstract metaphors of embodiment with their images of bodily fluids, they have expressed revulsion over Catherine's viscous evocation of the body and blood of a dying man. This says much about our modern ability to cope with the realities of corporeality, however much we might employ the rhetoric of the body in our academic musings.

II. Different meanings of body

1. The mortal body

There is a paradox running through the *Dialogue*, in so far as its themes of good and evil, obedience and sin, seem at first to be set up in opposition to one another, with the body and sensuality being identified primarily in negative terms. However, these contrasts have to be understood in the context of a more harmonious and reconciling vision, in which the struggle between the body and soul is ultimately resolved in their reunion in a state of bliss or damnation. In the resurrection, the soul receives her glorified body as a gift, and she in turn brings happiness to the body: 'Her own fullness will overflow when on the final day of judgment she puts on once more the garment of her own flesh, which she had left behind.'[9] But for souls that have resisted God's mercy, the body will share in the soul's torment, 'For the body was the soul's partner and instrument in doing good and evil as the will was pleased to choose.'[10]

Catherine's depictions of sin and damnation are replete with images of diseased and suppurating bodies, particularly when she is describing the corruption of priests and others who pollute the body of Holy Mother Church. However, in this too she does not lend herself to a univocal reading, because even her most vivid rhetoric of damnation has to be understood in the context of God's all-encompassing providence. Catherine's understanding of sin is of negation – sin 'is nothing'[11] – and God's desire to love and forgive his creatures overcomes every obstacle except that of pride, by which the sinner finally refuses to accept God's mercy. Catherine anticipates Luther in her understanding of God's grace as an infinite source of forgiveness that renders futile every finite human work. Indeed, she is sceptical of the value of bodily penances, emphasizing that only the will is capable of pleasing God.

But if for Catherine the body is an instrument of the soul that of itself plays no active role in salvation, it is nevertheless the body that allows the soul to express her love for God through love of neighbour. 'Every action, whether good or evil, is done by means of the body.'[12] This means that the body has the capacity to work in harmonious union with the soul:

> ... when the great chords of the soul's powers are harmonized, the small chords of the body's senses and organs are blended ... Every member does the work given it to do, each one perfect in its own way: the eye in seeing, the ear in hearing, the nose in smelling, the taste in tasting, the tongue in speaking, the hands in touching and working, the feet in walking. All are harmonized in one sound to serve their neighbours for the glory and praise of my name, to serve the soul with good, holy, virtuous actions, obediently responding to the soul as its organs.[13]

Catherine's mystical relationship with God is one of transcendence and ecstasy, but it is first and foremost one that must be actively expressed in neighbourly love. God tells her that 'every sin committed against me is done by means of your neighbours'.[14] She describes God's contempt for those who put their own spiritual consolation before their neighbour's need: 'they offend me more by abandoning charity for their neighbour for a particular exercise or for spiritual quiet than if they had abandoned the exercise for their neighbour.'[15] I would go so far as to say that there are two passions that drive Catherine's spirituality – the first is the longing of her soul for union with God, and the second is her profound sense of social and economic justice expressed in a radical concern for the poor. Time and again she puts into the mouth of God her own furious condemnation of those who, 'bloated with pride as they are . . . never have their fill of gobbling up earthly riches and the pleasures of the world, while they are stingy, greedy, and avaricious toward the poor'.[16]

But this theme too is played out in the context of a wider generosity and pragmatism. There is, Catherine's God insists, nothing wrong in enjoying the material goods of life so long as they are in their proper context: 'After all, everything is good and perfect, created by me, Goodness itself. But I made these things to serve my rational creatures; I did not intend my creatures to make themselves servants and slaves to the world's pleasures.'[17]

Again, this is a reminder that the material world – including the human body and its needs – is good because it is created by God. It is the human will that gives it ethical significance, depending on whether it is used for the good of humankind in general and particularly for the poor, or appropriated and consumed by the rich with no thought for their neighbours in need. There are many resonances between Catherine's mystical theology and liberation theology, and she offers no pious withdrawal from the ongoing challenge of social justice. But nor does she place impossible burdens upon others. It is for each of us to discern our vocation and to live in obedience to God's calling and in service to our neighbour, whatever our status or possessions.

2. The transcendent body

The mortal body is for Catherine a heaviness and a limitation to the soul, but at the same time the body provides an abundance of metaphors for the soul's relationship to God. Following on from Bynum's suggestion above, we need to read her mysticism not as a rejection or suppression of the body, but as a symbolic performance of the body that finds its perfection, delight and nourishment in Christ. Thus it is not the mortal and finite body that is capable of knowing God, but the imaginary body in ecstatic union with Christ. This union is described in both maternal and nuptial language. God is the 'mad lover' of the soul, 'drunk [with desire] for her salvation'.[18] The relationship between Christ and the soul is such that 'he makes of her another himself'.[19] At the same time, the soul 'has the Holy Spirit as a mother who nurtures her at the breast of divine charity'.[20]

Catherine does not offer us a set of abstract propositions or philosophical reflections about God. She constructs in words a divinized body that enjoys the most intimate possible union with God in Christ, and through her rhetoric of desire she pulls us towards this body so that it becomes, not simply her own soul in exclusive union with God, but the Christian body that transcends all its mortal particularities and contexts. This is why I think that there can be a rich encounter between modern theology and Catherine's *Dialogue*. Whatever our cultural contexts and questions, we all face the same ultimate questions if we are part of the story of Christ – questions that concern the nature of the relationship between our humanity and the incarnation, what we mean by the resurrection of the body, the mystery of the Trinity in relation to the human spirit, the form of God's love for us and of our response to that love, the ways in which that love can be expressed and lived out individually and collectively in the church and society. Our answers to these questions might not be the same as Catherine's, but the questions do not change.

3. The sacramental body

Catherine's soul is a symbolic body, but it would be wrong to interpret this strictly in terms of postmodern linguistic theory such as that offered by Jacques Derrida, Jacques Lacan and, to a lesser extent, Luce Irigaray, where the body is constructed entirely at the symbolic level with no significance accorded to the material body in its personal relationships and social contexts. In Catherine's theology, sacramentality provides a form of mediation, a connecting link between the transcendent, idealized body of the soul, and the mortal body itself. Through the sacraments, the body becomes a source of nourishment for the soul, and thus Catherine's language of sacramentality is informed by a symbolics of corporeality that fluctuates between the material and the spiritual. One passage in particular suggests the ways in which she weaves together images of spiritual embodiment to offer a reflection on the soul's transcendence, while at the same time rooting this in the body's physical reception of the eucharistic elements:

> And how, dearest daughter, should you and others look upon this mystery

and touch it? Not only with your bodily eyes and feeling, for here they would fail you . . . What tastes and sees and touches this sacrament? The soul's sensitivity . . . How does she see it? With her mind's eye, so long as it has the pupil of holy faith . . . How is this sacrament touched? With the hand of love . . . How is this sacrament tasted? With holy desire. The body tastes only the flavour of bread, but the soul tastes me, God and human . . . So you see, you must receive this sacrament not only with your bodily senses but with your spiritual sensitivity, by disposing your soul to see and receive and taste this sacrament with affectionate love.[21]

The difference therefore between Catherine's highly symbolic discourse of the soul, and postmodern theories of symbolism, is that hers is ultimately a sacramental rather than a symbolic body. It is physically incorporated into the body of the church through the body and blood of Christ, and it will ultimately share in the soul's resurrection through its perfection in the risen Christ. Thus the language she uses, although privileging spirituality over corporeality, nonetheless consistently relates its spiritual insights to the body's gestures, relationships and ways of behaving. Whereas postmodern linguistic theory makes language the site of a performative and mimetic existence divorced from the ethical and communal demands of living in the world, sacramentality seeks to embody the transcendent ideals of the imaginary body constructed in the language of redemption, within the material relationships and dependencies of corporeal existence.

III. Conclusion

There is much in Catherine's life and mysticism that can justifiably be criticized from a modern perspective. She reflects Christianity's hostility towards the body and its tendencies to foster extreme forms of female asceticism, and her rhetorical extremes tend to jar on modern sensibilities. Nevertheless, she also poses a challenge to modern theologians, in so far as she reminds us that theology is not an intellectual exercise but a mapping of the body – the personal body, the social body and the church's body – in such a way that the active love of one's neighbour in need becomes the motivation and the purpose of all Christian spirituality and practice. This is an unfashionable suggestion today, particularly among feminists who point out how often the church's tradition of service and self-sacrifice have been the exclusive domain of women. Nevertheless, when I think of those sisters living amongst and ministering to Zambia's dying and orphaned AIDS victims, I glimpse a living theology of the Christian body that is more eloquent and challenging than any written text.

Catherine teaches us how to go beyond the structured language of theory and rationalization, to a more fluid and dialogical discourse of embodiment, desire and transcendence that does not close its ears to the cry of the poor. The suffering body, the ecstatic body, the poor body, the desiring body, the resistant body, all these find a space of co-existence without denying the struggle inherent in the Christian quest for holiness of body and mind. She is not a saint for the faint-hearted, but she is perhaps a saint for those who seek a language than can express the lavish abundance of life in Christ, and the radical challenge of ministering to the poor in a world and a church so often marked by corruption, greed and excess. Catherine suggests ways in which the sacramental body – a body that is constructed in the space of flux between the mortality and suffering of the finite body, and the transcendence and joy of the soul – provides a language of anguish and desire, responsibility and freedom, that might provide a theological style as relevant for the twenty-first century as it was for mediaeval Siena.

Notes

1. Cf. Rebecca S. Chopp and Sheila Greeve Davaney (eds), *Horizons in Feminist Theology: Identity, Tradition, and Norms*, Minneapolis: Fortress Press 1997. This collection of essays generated considerable debate amongst feminist theologians – see 'Roundtable Discussion: From Generation to Generation' in *The Journal of Feminist Studies in Religion*, Vol. XV, No. 1, 1999, pp. 102–38.
2. See Melvyn Matthews, *Both Alike to Thee: The Retrieval of the Mystical Way*, London: SPCK 2000; Denys Turner, *The Darkness of God: Negativity in Christian Mysticism*, Cambridge: Cambridge University Press 1995; Rowan Williams, *Teresa of Avila*, London: Geoffrey Chapman 1991.
3. Edith Wyschogrod, *Saints and Postmodernism: Revisioning Moral Philosophy*, Chicago and London: University of Chicago Press 1990, p. 15
4. See Caroline Walker Bynum, *Holy Feast and Holy Fast: The Religious Significance of Food to Medieval Women*, University of California Press 1987; Grace Jantzen, *Power, Gender and Christian Mysticism*, Cambridge: Cambridge University Press 1995; see also Rudolph M. Bell, *Holy Anorexia*, Chicago and London: University of Chicago Press 1985.
5. Jantzen, *Power, Gender and Christian Mysticism*, p. 223.
6. Bynum, 'Women Mystics and Eucharistic Devotion' in *Fragmentation and Redemption: Essays on Gender and the Human Body in Medieval Religion*, New York: Zone Books 1992, pp. 142–3.
7. See *Saint Catherine of Siena as seen in her Letters*, translated and edited with an

introduction by Vida D. Scudder, London: J. M. Dent & Co. and New York: E. P. Dutton & Co. 1905, pp. 109–14.
8. Cf. Luce Irigaray, *This Sex Which Is Not One*, trs Catherine Porter with Carolyn Burke, Ithaca, NY: Cornell University Press 1985.
9. *Catherine of Siena: The Dialogue*, translated and with an introduction by Suzanne Noffke, OP, preface by Giuliana Cavallini, New York, Mahwah: Paulist Press 1980, p. 84.
10. Ibid, p. 8.6
11. Ibid, p. 142.
12. Ibid, p. 86.
13. Ibid, p. 310.
14. Ibid, p. 35.
15. Ibid, p. 131.
16. Ibid, p. 232.
17. Ibid, p. 97.
18. Ibid, p. 325.
19. Ibid, p. 25.
20. Ibid, p. 292.
21. Ibid, pp. 210–11.

The Immobile Dance:
The Body and the Bible in Latin America

NANCY CARDOSO PEREIRA

This mouth open in shock, joy, and fear. These eyes screwed up against the sun. This hand closed in a fist beating the air and this other hand open to ask. These feet planted on the ground, these feet expelled from the land, these feet scratched by the soil, these grounded, landless feet. These ears avid for silence and salsa, prayer and bolero, samba and passion, command and goal. This stomach full of tacos and beans, feasts and famines, sons and daughters of maize. These arms and legs of work and weariness, dance and sleep, unpayable debts. This African and Latin skin, as old as the Andes or Lake Zacatenco. This is my body. The bodies of Latin America.

I. Body: mirror and labyrinth

'The Immobile Dance',[1] a novel by the Peruvian writer Manuel Scorza, describes our Latin American struggles on the basis of this image made up of movement and immobility. Choosing; opting; deciding; taking a stand . . . There are two Peruvian militants in exile in Paris, preparing to return to the struggle in the Peruvian jungle. While they are waiting to go back, they get to know people and places; they become involved and need to choose between going back and leaving, staying and leaving:

> The novel is a counterpoint between a guerrilla fighter and an ex-guerrilla . . . a conflict between two men who have to choose between Love and Revolution. One chooses revolution, the other love. At the end of their lives, each believes the other made the better choice. Through a play of mirrors, each envies the other's life.[2]

One story inside another. Each makes his own choice: one stays and the other leaves . . . as if the exercise of choice always leaves a door half open to doubt.

This fixed pair that invalidates movement and immobilizes the dance forms part of our most cherished traditions of struggle. These are new old discourses, which rebuild the tradition of denying the pleasure-seeking body as a condition for building up the fighting body. One way or another, the old dualism pursues us like a sign, endlessly repeating what people say. Che Guevara said: 'Everyone has the right to get tired, but those who get tired are not leaders.'

A good dose of the religious traditions of Christianity and of biblical imagery – understood as part of the dominant Western culture and science – feeds this devouring hunger for choices and their fixed pairs. It is an epistemological and an ethical dualism at the same time,[3] which organizes reality and relationships in the form of opposites, conferring positive value on only one of the terms. In this scheme of things, freedom is always hostage to the good/evil binomial, as though the truth of choice were outside ourselves and as though there were a secure and objective place outside the body and against the body that founds and upholds truth, or discernment, or justice.

By making the body a place of error we again stand naked before the divinity, accused of desiring. We are then clad in a theology that covers up the body and its hidden places: pockets of priorities, stitches of sacrifice, necklines of obedience, buttons of rules, and a false hem to hide the excesses of desire.

The quest for alternatives cannot be understood as affirmation of the autonomous body as expression of a liberal individualism hiding the social constructs that shape the structures of language and of power. It is an attempt to break with the paralysing impasse that makes us have to choose, ever and again, between the individual and the collective, between passionate senses and reason, between technology and sensitivity. It is an attempt to affirm bodies as *loci* of interpretation, text, and reading of the world and its relationships.

In metaphysics, the body is a prop for consciousness, thereby isolating it from the dynamic of understanding, from reflective discourse, reducing it to an object to be studied. Broadening the act of understanding to take in the body does not mean affirming it as the starting point or safe foundation for thought – which would simply be replacing a 'metaphysical sleep' with an 'anthropological sleep'.[4]

The hermeneutical proposal is to modify our understanding of understanding. The body is not an envelope for consciousness, but it is the experience-event that destroys the dualism between essence and appearance, subjectivity and objectivity, activity and passivity, and other fixed binomials established by the patriarchal metaphysical tradition.

Re-creative hermeneutics is, of necessity, going to need to be a dialogue of suspicion and critique, a dialogue and argument with tradition and common sense. Because understanding means making choices, adopting a position including what is said and what is unsaid, the visible and the invisible, what is thought and what has not been thought. It is speech that questions itself, that understands at the same time as it clarifies its motives.

The reflecting body changes the nature of reflection and opens up spaces for meaning because it experiences the reversibility of the senses. The senses are not only a biological operation: they are also interpreters of the 'eye that touches, the hands [that] see, the eyes [that] move with touch, touch [that] upholds through the eyes our immobility and mobility . . .'.[5]

But we still listen to music . . . even without dancing. The skin-deep country still likes to show itself without having to choose between one thing and another. In both our Latin American novels and our militancy these hidden places are being confronted and taken over. For those who manage to love and to suspect their motives at the same time, the search for new ways of living that are integrated in and integrating of the body and its relationships becomes a collective exercise in interpretation, of fusion of outlooks, of manner of living.[6]

Recognizing the theological and pastoral compromises made by this literary and experiential dualism, creating alternatives, and daring to break the mould have been part of the pleasure and the duty of those who are doing theology in the feminine plural in Latin America:

'. . . it is essential to make politics and poetry. When a revolutionary is not a poet, he ends by being a dictator or a bureaucrat, a delator of his own dreams . . . On the end wall will still be written, "The Revolution must dwell only on happiness."'[7]

II. Body and Bible: the reverse side of the story of Lot's wife and daughters (Gen. 19)

We women are all like Lot's wife: a pain in the neck for not knowing how to listen! There we stand: immobilized and pickled in sulphur. Who said to look back? The way this woman was lost in the blink of an eye is forever fixed in history and our imagination. Left behind as a sculpture in homage to all other women – dead or alive – and their unfortunate choices. The world is being consumed in fire and wrath, and she . . . she chooses to turn round! Her husband is informed and organized, and she . . . ignorant or stupid, she looks back! Her neck moves in a barely perceptible turn, sideways and back at virtually the same instant. Her whole body rises into her eyes, trying . . . . What? Who knows? Neither her nor us, since no one has ever sought to learn what moved her body in that fatal moment of decision. Fulminating judgment. Deserved punishment. Pillar of salt. What haunts me and leaves me dissatisfied is trying to picture her posture, the movement of an immobilized body, a statue of a woman in movement at the exact moment of decision. Immobilized Venus. A solid yet insignificant fragment, the story of Lot's wife and her neck means very little . . . but there is the possibility of making the pillar of salt move for a second: a smile at the corners of her mouth as the wife hears from afar her two daughters deciding to get pregnant by their father. For one moment – of glory and revenge – she sighs with relief and shivers with the knowledge that the text a little further on immobilizes their father Lot – old and feeble – and leaves him at the mercy of the choice made by his daughters: a little wine and so to lie with their father without his knowledge, get pregnant, and engender two nations. And so every family has a little bit of transgression and a little bit of salt.

1. 'Our father is old and there is not a man on earth to come in to us . . .'
(Gen. 16.23–38)

The women conduct the whole narrative. They evaluate, decide, plan, execute, re-evaluate and go right to the end to ensure there is no end – to carry on life. The limitations are clear: there is no man. Their father: old! There is no sex, so no conception, no people, no life.

It is a story about the world coming to an end. The recollection of a world ending in fire and sulphur. Another narrative tells of the world ending in water (Gen. 6–10). In the accounts of the Flood, the protagonists are men, tillers of the soil. Noah and God evaluate and plan how to conserve life, and they carry out the plan of the ark on the flood waters. The re-creation here is to come about on the basis of remnants of the old social order that has been destroyed: a nucleus of the patriarchal family (see Gen. 7.7).

The story in Genesis 19 is also that of a world ending, the world of the cities of Sodom and Gomorrah. But the materials of the old order are not to hand: the patriarchal family and its capacity to give life are also to be consumed in the fire. The father is old. There are no men. Nor God. The mother, prisoner of the old order/choice of the father, has been left behind immobilized: a pillar of salt (19.26). The daughters are left. Women.

Here the *genesis* is decided by women. They make themselves fecund. They take semen from the old father, drunk and unconscious, and so take control of the capacity to choose and begin again. In the previous pericope (19.7–8) the daughters are entirely at the disposal of the father's choices: Lot offers his daughters to the men of the city in an attempt to prevent them from abusing two guest-messengers and thereby to uphold the code of hospitality, an important aspect of the patriarchal family.

Now, however, things are different . . . The destruction of the old order of Sodom and Gomorrah includes that of the patriarchal codes and their power to rule. Now it is the women who evaluate and decide. The father is at the daughters' disposal: it is they who take charge of the father's sex. They are sexually active: not only are they concerned with procreation but (in verse 31) they want learn about sex, while in the next verse they are concerned to 'preserve offspring'. In any case, it is they who decide and who take the initiative.

The text describes a situation of crisis and ending in which the body of the earth smokes and contorts under divine judgment. Then the two sisters feel the pain of loss, which encourages them to take the risk of choosing. Daughters of their mother – a pillar of salt raised from the ground – they turn not just their necks but their whole bodies. They rise up in the movement of evaluating and deciding. They take the risk – all the risks of tradition and of common sense. The devise the music and dance to it.

2. *What we need to know about sex to understand the text*

Two words are used in the text to speak about sex: *bv'*, to come in, to arrive, to cohabit, and *shkb*, to lay down, to lie with, to cohabit, ejeculation, sexual act. 'Laying down' or 'lying with' are prominent in Genesis 19, appearing six times. This is the same term as that used by Leviticus to condemn illicit sexual relations (Lev. 14; 15; 18; 20). In the story of Lot's daughters, the terms are alternated and repeated but applied exclusively to the actions of the women. The Book of Ruth – in which a woman also takes a strong lead – is also prolific in *lying with* (eight times) and *coming in* (six times).

The presence of wine is basic to this text. In the Bible, wine is present in various scenarios, with a frequent connection made with lack of understanding and strong sensuality: see Hosea 4.11; Song of Songs 1.2–4, 4.10, 5.1, 7.10, 8.2. In Esther 1.10, Judith 12.10ff., and Ruth 3.7 wine is explicitly linked to seduction and loss of control of the situation on the part of men.

According to Leviticus 18, sexual relations with one's father or mother – incest – are forbidden. The prohibitions are directed at the *man*, which is consistent with the view that sexual initiative is entirely masculine, which does not – formally – bind women. The list is detailed but leaves some disconcerting gaps: there is no specific prohibition in relation to the father who uncovers his daughter's nakedness. The text forbids sexual relations with 'your son's daughter or your daughter's daughter', that is, your granddaughter. As for female initiative, the text speaks only of a woman 'giving herself to an animal to have sexual relations with it' (v. 23), adding that this is 'perversion'! So, what with gaps and details, the text shows the area of sexuality as a battlefield, on which women also could play an autonomous part. The introduction to Leviticus 18 gives as justification for forbidding incestuous relationships; 'you shall not do as [other nations] do', thereby trying to guarantee Israel a more worthy origin than that of other peoples.

3. Not afraid of choosing music and dance – back to Genesis 19

The text involves the question of annulling the father. In verse 30 Lot is still taking the initiative. From verse 31 on it is they – the daughters – who take control of the situation. Lot does not *know* what is happening. In a cave, up in the hills, far from the world of the father and his rules, women take charge and assume control over sexual relations, reproduction, and social organization.

The text is repetitive. Actions are repeated in the consensus between the two women, with the leadership of the elder, the ancestress of the Moabites, emphasized. The Bible speaks of another Moabite – Ruth – who takes the intiative in sexual and reproductive matters in a relationship with an old man (Ruth 3.10) – another man who does not realize what is happening in that night of drinking and 'contented mood'. On the initiative of the Moabite Ruth – worked out with Naomi – life is preserved and justice upheld (4.14). Would it be possible to bring the memories of these women, of their decisions and struggles, closer? They are memories of life being redeemed on the basis of actions and decisions taken by women outside the limits of paternal order.

The women of Genesis are in a patriarchal mould, but they are remembered for their autonomous initiatives and the power of their decisions, which change the course of the family history, as Rebekah does in 27.6. The way women manage political processes, their relationships in the domestic sphere, and control of reproductive processes, basic to the narratives of the origins of the nation or nations in the Bible, should critique and reinterpret the existing patriarchal readings. These women are neither victims nor idealized heroines; they are a constituent part of the memories of the many origins of many nations: Sarah of Isaac, Keturah of Abraham's sons in the 'east country', Hagar of Ismael, Lot's daughters of Moab and Benammi,

Rachel and Lia of the sons/tribes of Jacob. Perhaps – who knows? – relearning to tell the story of our origins in the feminine plural might lead to finding alternative reasons for tolerance and co-existence among the different traditions.

While the story of Lot's daughters has traditionally been taken as a text condeming the origins of the Moabite and Ammonite peoples, linking them to a dubious and illegal origin, re-reading the text as the story of the choice made by the daughters would let us appreaciate the sympathy it shows to them. It makes no reference to sin or curse. The narrative insists on the need to preserve life. What seems likely is that patriarchal scholarship has tried to place Genesis 19.30ff. in the frame of taboos relating to incest, while the text itself makes no adverse judgment on the behaviour of the women. The underlying memory is affirmative and supportive of the mothers of the Moabites and Ammonites.

III. Conclusion: an invitation to the dance

Between the immobilized mother and the dance of *coming in and lying down* by the daughters there yawns an enormous space for building possibilities, for reading the Bible and life in affirmation of bodies in relation to one another as the setting for revelation, criticism and poetry, culture and passion.

To do this we need to learn to read words about the body in their concreteness and materialities, their symbolism and imagery. Identifying movements and immobility may help us to perceive biblical memories in their dynamic of creative conflict, moving beyond the patriarchal framework of interpretation, which punishes choices and immobilizes the text. This hermeneutical challenge speaks to women's movements and their struggles, particularly in the sphere of affirming and developing a feminist ethics and of re-appropriating and controlling what we – we women – are capable of producing and creating, both on the symbolic level (the sacred, divinities, beginnings and ends . . .) and in the reproductive and political material spheres.

The structures of violence and deprivation that mark the Latin American body tell us that the choice has already been made and that outside the globalized market there is no salvation.[8] They isolate bodies, choose some bodies, exclude the majority. Living in Latin America means always and again living the conflict and confrontation of not letting oneself be seduced by the wrong choices of the Empire, which take us far from what we love and from our liberation struggles. Scorza's peasant war is still going on, and the country inside our skin still rouses us to sensitivity and daring, joy and irreverence, spirituality and militancy here to the south of the Equator.

> I know you
> won't believe me,
> but it sings,
> the salt sings,
> the skin of the salt mines
> sings through a mouth smothered in earth.
> I shivered in that wilderness
> when I heard the salt's voice
> in the desert.
>
> *Pablo Neruda*[9]

Far off, the salt statue stirs and rises no longer like an immobile monument to punishment and loss . . . It is now a standing stone to some resistant goddess, a homage to risk, a eulogy to the giddiness of choice. God with us.

Translated by Paul Burns

Notes

1. Manuel Scorza, *A dança imóvel*, Rio de Janeiro 1984.
2. Ibid., p. 20.
3. Ivone Gebara, *Rompendo o silêncio – uma fenomenologia feminista do mal*, Petrópolis 2000, p. 117.
4. Michel Foucault, *As palavras e as coisas*, São Paulo 1979, p. 354.
5. Merleau-Ponty, *O visível e o invisível*, São Paulo 1976, p. 134.
6. Hans-Georg Gadamer, *Verdad y Método*, Salamanca 1997, p. 376.
7. Ibid., p.51.
8. Elsa Tamez, *La teología del éxito en un mundo desigual*, Quito 1998, p. 26.
9. Pablo Neruda, 'Oda a la sal' (Ode to Salt) in *Odas elementales*, Buenos Aires, 1954. The original reads:

> Sé que usted
> no me creerá,
> pero canta,
> la sal canta,
> la piel de las minas de sal canta
> con una boca sofocada por la tierra.
> Temblé en esas soledades
> cuando oí la voz de la sal
> en el desierto.

Cosmos – Church – Body: Observations on the Notion of 'Healing Pastoral Work'*

RAINER BUCHER

I. The prehistory

If in fact 'three main spheres of human experience' govern our existence, more specifically 'the experience of the body', 'community' and 'the cosmos',[1] then the course of church pastoral power[2] would manifestly lead from the cosmos to community – and at present leads to the body. Whereas the way in which Christianity seemed as a matter of course to be coded into the cosmos dissolved in the paradigm shifts of the disciplines in the eighteenth and early nineteenth century with the emancipation from religion, and (at least for the Catholic Church) the social coding began increasingly to crumble and to develop gaps in the middle of the twentieth century – in the dissolution of its social form as a closed milieu – nevertheless the church remained and remains the place where the significance of the faith which it hands down is depicted.

Materially, however, that represents quite a break with its own tradition. For in this tradition, in clear contrast to the New Testament writings, while the body played an important role, it was a role with dominantly negative connotations.[3] The anthropological dualism which has prevailed in the history of Christianity 'teaches not only the falling apart of "body" and "soul", material and immaterial, but a kind of state of war between the two, a state of siege with surprise attacks on both sides: the ascetic attacks of the soul on the body, and the ecstatic sensual attacks of the body on the soul'.[4] That is now a thing of the past. The body and Christianity are at present arranging them-

---

* German has two words for pastoral work, *Pastoral* and *Seelsorge*, the latter meaning literally 'the care of souls'. They can be used interchangeably, and it would be more natural to translate them both in the same way throughout this article. However, towards the end the author makes an important distinction between *Pastoral* and *Seelsorge* in connection with Vatican II and here it is crucial that two different English terms should be used. For the sake of consistency throughout the article I have therefore translated *Seelsorge* as 'care of souls', even though there are passages where 'pastoral work' would sound better [Tr.]

selves in a completely new way in the developed societies. The concept which denotes this is 'healing care of souls'.⁵

II. The aim of healing care of souls

1. De-spiritualizing

'Healing care of souls' aims to revise a specific dogmatic shift with momentous pastoral consequences. According to Isidor Baumgartner, the intention is to reverse 'the christological shift from the healing Jesus to the Christ who gives salvation'.⁶ For in the church 'the effective power of the pre-existent and exalted Christ is no longer described as "healing" (*sozein*) but as salvation (*soteria*)'.

As a result of this, according to Baumgartner, healing is 'transferred to heaven and spiritualized in an subliminally monophysite christology. The message of the kingdom of God ceases to be near to life and becomes a matter for teaching and the confession.' Thus healing and liberation increasingly moved away 'from a pastoral work which was interested in eternal salvation and not in concrete healing and liberation'. The objection to this 'marginalization of healing and liberating praxis supported by half a christology' is that 'the church makes present the "Christ who lives on" in his totality only "if at the same time it embodies the Christ who lives on in a diaconia which can really be experienced"'.⁷

So 'healing pastoral work' seeks to overcome the split between salvation and healing, faith and life, mysticism and politics. 'In view of the activity of Jesus we have to learn again that God does not come on the other side of the practice of healing and liberation but in it.'⁸ The aim is an 'alternative Christian praxis which protests against subtle and open inhumanity and takes the side of the individuality of the person and the fragmentary nature that he or she may have, as this is expressed in Jesus' action for the kingdom of God'. Such healing 'raises its voice for those who have no power of definition'; it has its 'decisive matrix' in the healing and liberating action of Jesus himself.⁹

Now this self-definition of 'healing pastoral work', which sounds almost like liberation theology, finds its sphere of application above all in what is traditionally called 'the individual care of souls',¹⁰ though it is extended into that crowded transitional field between body and psyche, which is being worked in on the one hand by a whole circle of professional helpers of a richly differentiated therapy society,¹¹ and on the other by psychosomatic medicine.

If we leave aside the (marginal) phenomenon of a Protestant[12] or a Catholic[13] recourse to magical practices of healing and also generously overlook the broad areas where pastoral work, the psycho-market and kitsch are amalgamated in this field,[14] the notion of 'healing pastoral work' accepts the modern perspective on the body and its professional aspects. There is widespread agreement that the 'monopoly claimed for centuries by Christian churches and theology in matters of healing' already 'collapsed in the nineteenth century' and cannot 'simply be restored by current church efforts to develop a "theology of healing"'.[15] Eugen Biser, for example, also points out that 'it cannot in any way be concerned to win back the territory ceded to scientific medicine and to put itself on the side of the spiritual healers and those who pray for health'.[16]

2. Three basic findings

The notion of 'healing care of souls' can now certainly base itself on three findings, the combination of which must be why it is so attractive today. First, Jesus healed in the framework of his message of the kingdom of God[17] and in so doing he turned by preference to those people 'who were regarded as unbelievers, unclean or morally reprehensible'.[18] Through Jesus' healings 'the distortion of creation by the power of evil was disclosed and the sufferer was not seen as a sinner who was being punished but as the victim of circumstances and unjust power structures which caused illness, and which came about as a result of human apostasy from God'.[19] Now that means that 'the New Testament proclamation proves to be a promise of healing rooted in the body and capable of being experienced in the body. The fact that now the body and with it bodily well-being has fallen into disrepute robs the preaching of its roots'.[20]

Secondly, 'healing care of souls' is a form of pastoral work which realizes the constitutive diaconal dimension of church action, i.e. its dimension of aid and orthopraxy, in a specific and very concentrated way.[21] If it is to base itself on Jesus, the church must follow him in taking the side of the sufferers. Even in the darkest phases of its existence the church did not succumb to the cult of the healthy and strong body; it paid attention to the sick, suffering body.

Thirdly, the modern pluralization of discourse on the body has not closed this field to religion and 'secularized' it, but has opened up a complex area often occupied by rival claims in which the human longing for wholeness is always actualized and, because it is only partially satisfied, is also perpetuated. In the present day 'neither the priest nor the physician nor the therapist represents an unquestioned healing authority in Western cultures who escapes questioning'.[22] All together these produce discourses and practices which do not just respond to the human longing for healing, but also generate it.

The mutual interconnection between these three elements – recourse to Jesus, embedding in the diaconal project of the church and the capacity to meet up with needs for healing beyond a largely scientific and technical medicine, which are increasing rather than decreasing – must account for the success of the concept of 'healing pastoral work'.

None of the reasons, particularly not the last one, destroys this concept. For religion has functions; it is not only meaningless to think of it without functions but above all it makes it functionless. However, while religion has functions, it is not exhausted by them. In it there is always a specific surplus over and above any particular function.

According to Eckhard Nordhofen,[23] it is true of the Jewish-Christian tradition in particular that in a striking way its monotheism runs contrary to a religion which merely satisfies needs. For from its very beginnings this Christian-Jewish tradition has been stamped by the notion that a God attuned to human needs is self-made, and a self-made God is not a God, but an idol. The God of Christianity is always also the wholly other, the one who is remote, who does not act as people expect him to. He stands for healing but does not guarantee it; indeed sometimes he even strikes and causes disaster.[24]

III. Problems

1. The starting point: no identity safeguarded against crisis

The church's new grasp of the body which is represented by the concept of 'healing care of souls' is orientated on salvation (like any of its actions). But in distinction from former times salvation based on religion is not promised *against* the body, but *with* it and *in* it. Of course the thought-out notions of 'healing pastoral' care indicate the knowledge that 'healing' and 'salvation' have to be distinguished. Thus on the one hand there is 'no Christian talk of salvation outside the correlation of the expectation of salvation and the message of redemption', and therefore 'to confess Jesus Christ as our salvation is possible only in the paradigmatic languages and practices of the interpretation of the world and existence',[25] but on the other hand it is also true that 'the promise of salvation in Jesus Christ is . . . not the promise of an identity which is safeguarded against crisis, nor the promise of an addictive harmony and experience of totality. It is the practical and symbolic promise under the eschatological proviso that the appearance of being a foretaste of the consummation of salvation in the context of a creation through which a rift runs from top to bottom.'[26]

Other obvious problem-fields and dangers of the concept of 'healing care of souls' must be reflected in the conceptual design of the present scholarly outlines of 'healing pastoral work'. These include the possible division between the care of individual souls and social diaconia,[27] or the separation of the care of souls from preaching (of the word), the trivialization of the task of the church, which is always also prophetic, so that it becomes an everyday concern about a functionally inconspicuous life, or succumbing to the myth of identity and integrity.[28] The degree to which this happens even with popular authors in this sector can be doubted, but not verified here.

Still, the concept of 'healing care of souls' also raises some problems which cannot be removed simply by more concentrated reflection. These are all problems of the classic pastoral-theological interface between discursive and non-discursive practice,[29] in other words problems which emerge when one relates the concept to power structures. In detail these are the power of the grass roots, the power of the authority of the magisterium, and the power of those engaged in pastoral action itself. So the issue is the factual question of the real existence of 'healing care of souls', the question of the relationship of this notion to the binding concept of pastoral work arrived at in Vatican II, and thirdly the question of the way in which this care deals with the unavoidable problem of pastoral power.

2. *'Healing care of souls', more than a wish? (question 1)*

'Healing care of souls' formulates a notion. Whether there is such a thing is still an open question. What do exist are communities of books around extraordinary successful authors on the frontiers of spirituality, theology and counselling, and (unfortunately more marginal) elements in pastoral and psychological education in the areas of study of theology and vocational training. But what actual practice underlies the concept of 'healing care of souls' in everyday church action?

Manifestly the life of the church goes on more or less undisturbed by this notion, and at most the shelves of (religious) bookshops confirm the existence of a phenomenon of 'healing care of souls' at the grass-roots level. The power of this pastoral scheme to change practice seems more limited, unless one regards the general, thoroughly pastoral call to make the whole person and his or her integral wholeness the content of pastoral action, along with the fundamental readiness not to prolong the church's traditional scorn for the body, as themselves a contribution to a 'healing pastoral work'. This may differ in different areas, but it should not change the picture of a general failure to follow through the concept of 'healing pastoral work' in the broader sphere of church action.

It is no coincidence that this is the situation. For what is still largely not being done is to work out the church's history of guilt over the body in a consistent way. For many centuries the basis of the power of religion was power over the bodies of the grass roots. That is true of the power of discourse and definition and it is also true of the very direct power to touch and violate. This history of the church's power over the body has been inscribed in the collective memory of Western cultures. Unless it is worked through, any talk of 'healing care of souls' comes under the suspicion of winning victories in one of the most painful (also in the literal sense) fields of pastoral history in order to gain new relevance in times when Christianity is becoming irrelevant in broad areas.

Of course this charge cannot be made against those who have developed this notion out of diaconal commitment, and often particularly in view of the Christian history of guilt about the body, and who back it up in both scholarship and practice. But there can be no pastoral work from scratch, certainly not work which is sensitive to diaconia, which is what 'healing pastoral work' seeks to be and indeed notionally is. Pastoral revolutions which turn their back on their own history can never succeed. The shift from traditional contempt for the body to the body as a place to which positive theological significance within the Christian saving event is attributed would be a pastoral revolution. So here too there can be no new beginning unless there is a focus on the break and the pains that it has caused.

However, that leads into a wide area. As is well known, European Catholic theology in the twentieth century, a century which has really brought incomparable disaster to the men and women of Europe and adjoining regions, has essentially managed to go on with its work without taking account of this disaster. It has therefore failed in the light of the disaster. But this failure continues to have an effect as a power of resistance against the power of the disaster.

Does it know the reasons for this failure? Can it escape this failure without noting the reasons for it? Where has the European theology of the twentieth century in fact formulated acceptable answers to both the political, social and individual concerns and needs of this particular century?

Thank God, pastoral work, i.e. the action of the church in all its breadth, could not endure this lack of context as comprehensively as proved possible for academic theology. But is the notion of 'healing pastoral work' really rooted in the history of pastoral work and thus in the *sensus fidelium* of the people of God? What is there in this notion generally – in the everyday practice of the church – over and above the partial reception of psychological (and psychoanalytical) insights and the concern to believe in the saving power of faith?

Is 'healing pastoral work' more than a wish? A look at the grass roots and the personnel of the church forces us to ask this question.

3. The notional problem or the limits of the concept of the care of souls (question 2)

A look at the authority of the magisterium suggests yet another question. What is the relationship between the notion of 'healing care of souls' and the conciliar notion of the renewal of the church as presented in *Gaudium et Spes*? This question is directed above all towards the concept of the care of souls.

In the German language area the term 'care of souls' is still used more or less as a synonym for 'pastoral work'. But 'care of souls' is not 'pastoral work'. For 'pastoral work' is a magisterial concept defined at the Second Vatican Council which goes far beyond what is embraced by the classical concept of care of souls as the lifelong individual guidance of the souls of laity by clergy, a guidance which is orientated on salvation. As used before the Council the term 'care of souls' has Platonizing, clerical, patriarchal and paternalistic connotations. It describes the action of clergy (i.e. males) towards laity, orientated on the salvation of the soul and eternal salvation, action which so dominates the laity that it leaves them no scope for taking responsibility for themselves.

By contrast, at Vatican II 'pastoral work' is an overall term for the action of the church in the present in accordance with the gospel. It embraces traditional individual care of souls, but the Pastoral Constitution also contains themes which classically belong in Christian social teaching, as these relate to the political and social order. Above all pastoral work as understood by Vatican II is not the action of clergy towards laity within the church but an action of all in the church in and for the world orientated on the gospel and the signs of the time.[30]

In *Gaudium et Spes* pastoral work means that relationship in action of the church to the world which the people of God has to build up in the light of the gospel. Thus pastoral work is a criteriological concept, not a Platonizing, a paternalistic or a patriarchal one. For it is not directed towards 'souls' but towards the whole person; it starts from the fundamental perichoresis of church and world in pastoral work and from the pastoral activity of the whole people of God, men and women.

Of course 'healing care of souls' is not focussed only on the soul in a Platonizing way, nor does it take control of people in paternalistic way, nor is it practised only by males in a patriarchal way. It is concerned with the 'integral' and concrete saving efficacy of the gospel for all men and women. That is what this concept states on the basis of Vatican II. But precisely for this reason the uncritical use of the 'concept of care of souls' and its widespread identification with the concept pastoral work is surprising.

Thus the concept of 'healing care of souls' conceptually stands in a tradition which has been far more comprehensively overcome by the 'concept of pastoral work' in Vatican II than it can ever be by the term 'healing care of souls'. The dogmatic relevance of pastoral work and the pastoral relevance of dogmatics,[31] the abolition of the pre-conciliar constellation of inside and outside and the removal of any clerical and patriarchal connotations of the term care of souls are achieved more fundamentally with the concept of pastoral work in *Gaudium et Spes* than with the term 'healing care of souls'.

Now if healing is in fact a constitutive task of pastoral action, which no one will dispute, along with concepts like 'cooperative pastoral work' or '*communio* ecclesiology' this concept belongs among the growing series of concepts in pastoral theology which arise simply from putting an adjective before the noun which denotes a constitutive element of its content and therefore emphasizes the obvious. This can only mean that what is obvious in practice is anything but obvious (as in our case), or that the obvious cannot be identified as such. Both would indicate serious defects in church practice, and that is indeed the case.

'It cannot be concealed that the way to a church in which healing and liberating diaconia has priority over all other tasks still seems to be a long one.' Isidor Baumgartner is certainly right in making this remark. Given the failure to implement all the concepts of Vatican II, it may also be correct that the 'change that this brings to the face of the church' must be a 'dimension which intervenes more deeply in the life of the church than the Second Vatican Council did',[32] but conceptually that is not the case. For the power of the authority of the magisterium has here already overcome limits at which the practice of the church and also the notion of 'healing pastoral work' still threaten to come to grief. [33]

4. The problem of one's own power (question 3)

A third question remains. If, as I remarked at the beginning, the way of the church's pastoral power leads from the cosmos to the community and at present to the body, the fate of the first two stages must terrify the last. For these places have gone under as pastoral contexts because of the ambivalence of their power.

That is true both of the power of cosmological discourse, which came to grief because of its impotence in the face of the evidence produced by the scientists of early modernity, and of the power of a concentrated social form of the 'church' in the era of Pope Pius XII (1950–60), which collapsed in the second wave of modernization in Western societies following the Second World War (here above all because of free access to education and the integration of women into the market).

'Healing pastoral work' seeks to represent the relevance of faith anew in an old place, the body. The body is a place full of longings and emotions and therefore a powerful place. It is also a place which had in fact been passed on to the church – particularly in Western societies – because of the all-too-obvious human defects of a highly specialized medical industry. But like these two areas which have tended to be lost, the body too is an ambivalent place.

For what Regina Ammicht Quinn writes generally about the renaissance of the body also applies to 'healing pastoral work'. The 'body, which today has come back into the centre of interest, does not speak what is expected of it and hoped from it: the language of truth, authenticity and naturalness'.[34] The body is no longer a place which can be 'occupied' by religion clearly and without loss any more than the cosmos and society are.

Certainly not for Christianity, not only because its history of the body is essentially a history of guilt, but because it could have learned from the process in modern times in which it has lost power that a depiction of the faith cannot avoid the ambivalence of concretion and transcendence, of incarnation and betrayal, of impotence in power and power in impotence. On the contrary, it can exist only in this ambivalence today, 'after the death of God and man', when 'both pillars of theology, God and human beings' seem 'to be shaky foundations in the present-day order of things'.[35]

In the body, Christian pastoral work cannot avoid the ambivalence to which it all too clearly succumbed in its cosmological and social coding. Nor can it evade this place, any more than it can evade the fact that human beings exist in the cosmos or in society. In view of any failure of a pastoral work based on power it must seek its language and its competence in this failure.

So the question remains: what contribution does pastoral work have to make to the fact that men and women live in the body, which they would not have if there were no pastoral work? Hopefully concrete help and support in disaster. Certainly prayer, blessing and intercession. And perhaps really also the quest for that field which opens up in the borderland between body and psyche and which the notions of 'healing care of souls' explores. The Christian tradition also has to represent the belief that God does not just wait for us in the victory over suffering but already in the tomb of our despair at suffering. Not because he gives it 'meaning' but because he shares its meaninglessness.

Translated by John Bowden

Notes

1. R. Ammicht-Quinn, 'Rituale und Körperlichkeit', in ead. and S. Spendel (eds), *Kraftfelder. Sakramente in der Lebenswirklichkeit von Frauen*, Regensburg 1998, pp. 33–51: 46.
2. For this term see M. Foucault, 'Warum ich Macht untersuche? Die Frage des Subjekts', in H. L. Dreyfus and P. Rabinov, *Jenseits von Strukturalismus und Hermeneutik*, Frankfurt am Main 1987, pp. 234–50. On this, though with intentions which tend rather to run counter to Foucault, who is critical of the subject, see H. Steinkamp, *Die sanfte Macht der Hirten. Die Bedeutung Michel Foucaults für die Praktische Theologie*, Mainz 1999.
3. Cf. R. Ammicht-Quinn, *Körper – Religion – Sexualität. Theologische Reflexionen zur Ethik der Geschlechter*, Mainz 1999, pp. 116–37. See also E. Klinger, S. Böhm and T. Seidl (eds), *Der Körper und die Religion. Das Problem der Konstruktion von Geschlechterrollen*, Würzburg 2000.
4. Ammicht-Quinn, 'Rituale und Körperlichkeit' (n.1), p. 41.
5. Cf. with a quite different scientific claim W. Beinert (ed.), *Heil und Heilen als pastorale Sorge*, Regensburg 1984; E. Biser, *Theologie als Therapie*, Heidelberg 1995; I. Baumgartner, *Pastoralpsychologie. Einführung in die Praxis heilender Seelsorge*, Düsseldorf 1990; id., *Heilende Seelsorge in Lebenskrisen*, Düsseldorf 1992; J. Hanle, *Heilende Verkündigung*, Ostfildern 1997; C. Jacobs, *Salutogenese*, Würzburg 2000; W. Müller, *Heilende Seelsorge*, Mainz 2000.
6. I. Baumgartner, 'Heilende Seelsorge – ein verkehrtes Leitwort?', *Theologisch-praktische Quartalschrift* 145, 1997, pp. 238–44: 239f.
7. Ibid., 240. In the last sentence Baumgartner is quoting O. Fuchs, *Heilen und*

Befreien. Der Dienst am Nächsten als Ernstfall von Kirche und Pastoral, Düsseldorf 1990, p. 86.
8. Ibid., p. 240.
9. Ibid., p. 244.
10. We might also recall 'pastoral medicine' as a transitional zone between pastoral work and medicine which was established at one time. The church's authority over the body first collapsed in the discussions of scientific medicine in the nineteenth century and its remnants came to grief in the discussions of psychotherapy in the twentieth. For the history of the body before the twentieth century see P. Sarasin, *Reizbare Maschinen. Eine Geschichte des Körpers 1765–1914*, Frankfurt am Main 2001.
11. For the characteristics of the 'therapy society' and its (social and ethical) problems see K. Remele, *Tanz um goldene Selbst. Therapiegesellschaft, Selbstverwirklichung und Gemeinwohl*, Graz, Vienna and Cologne 2001.
12. Cf. e.g. W. Margies, *Heilung durch sein Wort* (2 vols), Urbach 1983/85.
13. Thus for example in specific healing practices of African churches, but also on the periphery of the mainstream European Catholic Church. For this cf. e.g. the relevant Roman guidelines with which the Congregation of Faith is evidently attempting to incorporate healing rituals which are actually practised back into the context of the mainstream church. The Congregation of Faith instructs that in the course of services of healing 'anything resembling hysteria, artificiality, theatricality, or sensationalism must not take place' and it is important for it to point out that 'the "charisma of healing" . . . cannot simply be attributed to a particular category of the faithful' (Instruction on Prayers for Healing of 23 September 2000, accessible under www.vatican.va). For Africa see E. de Rosy, *Heilkunst in Afrika*, Wuppertal ²1998; M. Ott, *Jesus and the Witchdoctor – Jesus und der Wudnerheiler*, Würzburg 2001. For the term 'catholical' see K. Gabriel, *Christentum zwischen Christentum und Postmoderne*, Frankfurt am Main, Basel and Vienna 1992, pp. 196–8.
14. 'There is the pastoral literature and practice of a pseudo-poetic vulgarized neo-religious holiusm with its claim to inwardness' – thus Heribert Wahl in '"Alles ist Fragment" – aber Fragmente sint nicht alles! Rückfragen eines Pastoraltheologe und Psychoanalytikers', *Theologisch-Praktische Quartalschrift* 145, 1997, pp. 245–55: 254f. Wahl aptly continues: 'but that must not be confused with the paradigm of a "theory and practice of the care of souls with an analytical orientation".'
15. H.-G. Heimbrock, 'Heilung als Re-Konstruktion von Wirklichkeit. Kulturelle Aspekte eines Problems moderner Seelsorgelehre', in id. and W.-E. Failing, *Gelebte Religion wahrnehmen. Lebenswelt – Alltagskultur – Religionspraxis*, Stuttgart, Berlin and Cologne 1998, pp. 256–74.
16. E. Biser, 'The Healing Power of Faith. Outline of a Therapeutic Theology', *Concilium* 1998/5, pp. 68–78: 73.

17. Cf. H. K. Nielsen, *Heilung und Verkündigung. Das Verständnis der Heilung und ihres Verhältnisses zur Verkündigung bei Jesus und in der ältesten Kirche.*, Leiden, New York, Copenhagen and Cologne 1987; P. Trummer, *Die blutende Frau. Wunderheilung im Neuen Testament*, Freiburg im Breisgau 1991; id., *Dass meine Augen sich öffnen. Kleine Biblische Erkenntnislehre am Beispiel der Blindenheilungen Jesu*, Stuttgart 1998.
18. M. Pindl, *Versöhnung mit dem Leiden*, Frankfurt am Main, etc. 1998, p. 209.
19. O. Betz, 'Heilung/Heilungen, Neues Testament', *TRE* XIV, pp. 763–8: 766f.
20. Ammicht-Quinn, *Körper – Religion – Sexualität* (n.3), p. 135.
21. For diaconal theology, which has developed impressively in recent years above all in the German-speaking sphere see, H. Steinkamp, *Diakonie – Kennzeichen der Gemeinde*, Freiburg im Breisgau 1985; O. Fuchs, *Heilen und befreien. Der Dienst am Nächsten als Ernstfall von Kirche und Pastoral*, Düsseldorf 1990; H. Haslinger, *Diakonie zwischen Mensch, Kirche und Gesellschaft*, Würzburg 1996.
22. Heimbrock, 'Heilung als Re-Konstruktion von Wirklichkeit' (n.15), p. 267.
23. E. Nordhofen, *Der Engel der Bestreitung*, Würzburg 1993.
24. M. Görg, *Der un-heile Gott. Die Bibel im Bann der Gewalt*, Düsseldorf 1995.
25. F. Gruber, 'Heilwerden im Fragment. Anmerkungen zur heilenden Seelsorge aus systematischer Perspektive', *Theologisch-Praktische Quartalschrift* 145, 1997, pp. 227–37: 228, 227.
26. Ibid., p. 235.
27. Cf. here the remarks by K. H. Ladenhauf, 'Ihr werdet Aufatmen finden für euer Leben', in H. Windisch (ed.), *Seelsorge neu gestalten*, Graz 1995, pp. 35–58, which shows sensitive to the problem here.
28. These accusations are made e.g. by H. Poensgen in his polemic against 'healing care of souls', 'Alles ist Fragment. Kritische Anfragen zum Konzept heilender Seelsorge in der Pastoral', *Theologisch-Praktische Quartalschrift* 145, 1997, pp. 227–37. In this context it is also worth noting the questions raised by Ulrich Bach, who in connection with handicapped people writes: 'Those who make theological remarks about health and sickness . . . about salvation and healing, are criminally negligent if they do not at least now and then allow the question: what could my remarks mean for people who are much more strikingly affected by the topic of my statements than I am?', *'Heilende Gemeinde'. Versuch, einen Trend zu korrigieren*, Neukirchen-Vluyn 1988, p. 62.
29. For this genuine issue in pastoral theology see R. Bucher, 'Wer braucht Pastoraltheologie wozu? Zu den aktuellen Konstitutionsbedingungen eines Krisenfaches', in id. (ed.), *Theologie in den Kontrasten der Zukunft*, Graz 2001, pp. 181–97.
30. For the Council's concept of pastoral work see E. Klinger, *Armut – eine Herausforderung Gottes. Der Glaube des Konzils und die Befreiung des Menschen*, Zurich, Einsiedeln and Cologne 1990, pp. 96–134.
31. E. Klinger, 'Der Glaube des Konzils. Ein dogmatischer Fortschritt', in id. and

K.Wittstadt (eds), *Glaube im Prozess*, Freiburg im Breisgau, Basel and Vienna 1984, pp. 615–26.
32. Baumgartner, 'Heilende Seelsorge – ein verkehrtes Leitwort?' (n.6), p. 244.
33. The fact that the progress made at Vatican II in its historical analyses, its liberal interpretations and its revision of the practice of canon law, risk being lost to such a degree does not change the matter.
34. Ammicht Quinn, *Körper – Religion – Sexualität* (n.3), p. 136.
35. H.-J.Sander, 'Gott in den Fragmenten der Zeit. Systematische Theologie vor der Macht von Gottes und des Menschen Tod', in R. Bücher (ed.), *Theologie in den Kontrasten der Zukunft*, pp. 51–67: 50. See also H.-J.Sander, *Macht in der Ohnmacht. Eine Theologie der Menschenrechte*, Freiburg im Breisgau, Basel and Vienna 1999.

III. Intercultural Experiences

The Western Understanding of the Body as a Global Perspective

FARIDEH AKASHE-BÖHME

Cartesianism

The dominant view of the body in the West is a variant of Cartesianism. That already has two implications for the question whether this view can make universalist claims. On the one hand it is a historical product of the seventeenth century, and on the other hand, while it is indeed dominant in the West, it is by no means the only possible view. Therefore it makes sense first of all to consider the problems facing the Cartesian view of the body which have already been experienced by Western culture and indeed are still being experienced. Then I shall investigate what the globalization of this view of the body could mean in the conflict with other cultures.

The philosopher Descartes conceived of the human being as a combination of two substances, the *res extensa* and the *res cogitans*, the body and the soul. This is to understand the body as a machine the functioning of which is ultimately to be derived from mechanical interactions. As a substance, in what it is the body is independent of other substances, except God; in particular that also means an independence of the soul. In principle it is possible to think of organisms without souls; thus for example Descartes denies that animals have souls.

This viewpoint could initially be understood only as an epistemological model. As such, however, it has become extremely effective; indeed we can probably say that it was only on the basis of this notion of the body that modern scientific medicine could develop. For on the one hand that aroused the expectation that the essential details of what happens to the body can be recognized by objectifying methods, i.e. through access from outside and with instruments. Secondly, this approach removed the burden of all ideological scruples and ethical concerns which could have obscured or restricted dealings with the human body.

But Cartesianism is by no means just an epistemological model; rather, it is a cultural practice. The majority of men and women in Europe and North America not only think in Cartesian terms but also live in Cartesian terms. That begins with the medication they take every day to control bodily functions, continues with the progressive technologizing of the body, and ends with the legal safeguarding of organ transplants by the concept of brain death: the body which has no thought no longer enjoys the protection of human rights. Thus in the West Cartesianism has found its way deep into forms of life and cultural practices, in ways of dealing with sickness and health, in attitudes to physical work, in spheres like cosmetics and sport, and finally in the legal regulations which relate to all these spheres.

Globalization

The Cartesian view of the body is nowadays more than just a European or Western speciality. Rather, for about 150 years there has been a tendency to globalize this concept of the human body. This globalization takes place essentially through the dissemination of Western, i.e. scientific, medicine. And precisely in this way this concept of the body is disseminated by the practice of European forms of sport, e.g. in the framework of the Olympic movement: this happens implicitly with Western forms of life generally. Finally, the globalization of technology and industrial forms of work also transport the understanding of the body which they necessitate. One might think, for example, of Taylorism and the rationalization of industrial work by time and motion studies.

It is above all the victorious course of modern medicine which has established an objectivistic relationship to our bodies all over the world. Western medicine is not *per se* superior to other types of medicine, but it is superior in specific respects. It isolates the human body from connections with its environment and from social and biographical contexts and thus allows causes and effects to be directed. It is by fighting against infectious diseases and preventing them by inoculation, by directing systems through hormones, and above all by technological interventions like reproductive and transplantation medicine that Western medicine demonstrates its superiority. All these medical practices presuppose an approach to the human body under the eye of the physician or the natural scientist, i.e. from outside. Therefore the fundamental disciplines of this medicine are anatomy and physiology.

The second type of practice by which the Western concept of the body is globalized consists in the forms of work and transport which the industrial world makes necessary. Here the body is always understood as an instrument and treated accordingly. In order to remain inconspicuous in everyday activities, like a tool it must show the effectiveness expected in its particular state of life. On the one hand this attitude has led to a very widespread direction of bodily functions in everyday life – notably in the state of health – and on the other hand to general fitness training. This way of treating one's own body, which really belongs to the world of work with its expectations of high achievement; the compulsion for discipline, for independence from times and seasons and modes, has also meanwhile come to include the sphere of so-called leisure. Here too the body is not given its due. Rather, it is made the basis for particular achievements.

That brings up the theme of the third area in which the concept of body dominant in the West is being globalized today: the appearance of the body or the body as an essential part of the way in which we present ourselves. Granted, cosmetics and dressing up, jewellery and adornment, are as old as human cultural history, but in the West a special fashion in dress and appearance has developed which is specifically associated with the Western concept of the body. A combination of fashion with fitness techniques and medical techniques has also established the objectivistic concept of the body in the sphere of beauty. Here too the body is understood and treated merely as an instrument: an instrument which is meant to perform certain functions or produce certain effects. Thus cosmetic surgery and fitness studios have become a medium for initiation into Western notions of the body all over the world.

European alternatives

The objectivizing relationship to the body which developed in Cartesianism may be the dominant one in Europe, but it is by no means the only conception of the body. Rather, with the nineteenth century alternatives developed, both in thought and also in the form of life. Thus philosophy after Schopenhauer and Nietzsche made a discovery about the body which in the framework of the phenomenological movement led to wide research into bodily experiences. The body is a subjective given. This concept of a body from within was matched in practice by attention to the body in the framework of the life form movement around 1900.¹ This movement included sexual reform, reforms in food and clothing, and naturist culture. The idea of being natural had become the leading idea of these reform movements. In the face of the pressures of civilization and recourse to objectivizing natural sciences, nature was to be given back its rights. Understandably these efforts were mainly made in the sphere of the relationship of human beings to their bodies, in so far as 'the body is the nature that we ourselves are'.² There is no doubt that such efforts towards alternative forms of life were also time and again commandeered by the dominant economy and themselves became a variant of thinking in terms of achievement. Here the transformation of naturist culture through the keep-fit movement in Fascism into the body-building culture of the present is characteristic. On the other hand the efforts to achieve a non-objectivistic relationship to the body through the influence of Asian practices of self-cultivation have meanwhile been considerably reinforced.

Alternatives outside Europe

In an age of globalization bodies and images of bodies are no longer limited historically or culturally; even Western images of bodies are subject to other, new influences. Here we might think of the various practices of Yoga, of Tai Chi and Chi Gong, and indeed of Japanese martial arts, Confucian practices of self-cultivation and finally non-European traditions of medicine, especially Chinese medicine. Since these traditions have already gained such significant influence in Europe and North America, we may expect that in future they will also represent a counterbalance to the globalization of Western concepts of the body in other parts of the world. At least here a complementary relationship might be expected, in the sense that the one view compensates for the narrow-mindedness of the others. However, it could also be the case that conditions elsewhere settle down as they have now done in Europe and North America, where Asian practices relating to the body are used to compensate for or to prevent the damage done by an instrumentalized relationship to the body.

That would reduce these practices to mere bodily techniques and rob them of their spiritual background. Quite different ways of developing non-Western bodily practices might be conceivable over and above their mere function as compensation: they could develop into resistance against the globalization of the European concept of the body. Thus for example it is reported that the Confucian tradition in Japan has essentially prevented the establishment of transplant medicine there.[3] What could this mean for the Western world with its conflict over biomedicine, stem cells and pre-implantation diagnosis? In this sense the future is wide open.

Translated by John Bowden

Notes

1. *Die Lebensreform. Entwürfe zur Neugestaltung von Leben und Kunst um 1900*. Exhibition Catalogue, Darmstadt 2001.
2. Gernot Böhme, 'Leib: die Natur die wir selbst sind', in id., *Naturlich Natur. Über Natur im Zeitalter ihrer technischen Reproduzierbarkeit*, Frankfurt am Main ³1997.
3. William R. LaFleur, 'From Agape to Organs. Religious Differences between Japan and America in Judging the Ethics of the Transplant', in Joseph Runzo and Nancy M. Martin (eds), *Ethics in the World Religions*, Oxford 2001, pp. 271–90.

Bodies and Gender in Mesoamerican Religions

SYLVIA MARCOS

Introduction

Concepts of the body, its metaphors, bodily constraints and eroticism in Mesoamerican religious thought are embedded in gender and culture. By 'Mesoamerican religious thought', I am referring to the highly developed complex of perceptions, ideas and beliefs that constituted the epistemological framework of the Nahuas, the Mayas as well as of the other peoples of Mesoamerica.

The main sources for the present study are Books III and VI of the *General History of the Things of New Spain (Florentine Codex).*[1] Researchers have pointed out their depth and richness (especially of Book VI), and their value in bringing us closer to the moral vision and thought of the ancient Nahuas. Excerpts from the *Royal Palace Matritense Codex* and especially León-Portilla's recent translation of it were also examined.

Modern scientific certainties are not universals but are themselves historical constructions. This understanding permits a less confined way of looking at the Mesoamerican world. From this perspective, the biology – culture divide (or gender – sex divide) proves inadequate for approaching this universe. The concepts of duality, equilibrium, and fluidity are integral components of the Mesoamerican universe and essential to an understanding of corporality.

I. Duality in the Mesoamerican universe

The feminine-masculine dual unity was fundamental to the creation of the cosmos, its (re)generation, and sustenance. The fusion of feminine and masculine in one bi-polar principle is a recurring feature of Mesoamerican religious thinking. This principle, both singular and dual, is manifested by representations of pairs of gods and goddesses, beginning with Ometeotl, the supreme creator whose name means 'double god' or dual divinity.[2]

Dwelling beyond the thirteen heavens, Ometeotl was thought of as a feminine-masculine pair.

Omecihuatl and Ometecutli are the feminine and masculine halves of the divine duality Ometeotl. According to an ancient Nahua myth, they had a fight during which they broke dishes, and from every shard that hit the ground a new dual divinity sprang up. While some Mexicanists have inferred that this legend explains the multiplicity of gods, it also illustrates how the prime duality in its turn engenders dualities. Perhaps, then, gender itself – the primordial, all-pervasive duality – could be viewed as 'engendering' the multiple specific dualities underlying all phenomena.

Mesoamerican cosmology implied a concept of duality that was not fixed or static but constantly changing. An essential ingredient in Nahuatl thought, this motility gave its impulse to everything. Divinities, people, objects, time, and space with its five directions, had gender: they were feminine or masculine in proportions which continually changed. Gender, permeating all areas of nature, was itself the movement that engendered and transformed all identity.

In a cosmos so constructed, there would be little space for pyramid-like 'hierarchical' ordering and stratification. In the various Nahua narratives, whether we look at the *ilamatlatolli* (discourses of the wise old women), the *heuhuetlatolli* (discourses of the old men) or review sources that speak of pairs of deities, we can never infer any categorizing of one pole as 'superior' to the other. Instead, a sustaining characteristic of this conceptual universe seems to be the unfolding of dualities. This elaboration of dualities manifests itself on all levels of heaven, earth and below the earth as well as at the four corners of the universe.[3] The continuous unfolding is always in a state of flux, and is never rigidly stratified or fixed. Thus, duality permeated the entire cosmos, leaving its imprint on every object, situation, deity, and body.

Within this fluidity of metaphorical dualities, divine and corporeal, the only essential configuration was the mutual necessity to interconnect and interrelate. In the Mesoamerican universe, above and below did not imply superior and inferior. Not even in good and evil, nor between the divine and earthly, nor in death and life did hierarchical values stratified into superior and inferior exist. Life, for example, is born from death:

> Life and death interplayed on Great Mother Earth, forming a cycle of complementary opposites: life carried within it the seed of death; but without death rebirth was impossible because death was the pregnancy from which life emerged.[4]

According to Jacques Soustelle, '[t]he law of this world is the alternation of distinct qualities, radically separated, which dominate, disappear and reappear eternally . . .' .[5] In the universe, feminine and masculine attributes weave together in the generation of fluid, non-fixed identities. The shifting balance of opposing forces that made up the universe, from society to the body itself – as its reflection and image – should be understood as a manifestation of this interpenetration of genders. From the cosmos to the individual body, dual gender is revealed as the fundamental metaphor of Mesoamerican thought. It is reflected in the plasticity and dynamism that characterize its poles and that keep them "pulsating" as it were.[6]

Thus, Mesoamerican duality cannot be a binary ordering of 'static' poles. The idea of 'balance' can best be understood as an 'agent' that constantly modifies the terms of dualities and thereby bestows a singular quality on the opposite and complementary pairs that permeate all of Mesoamerican thought. It endows duality with flexibility or plasticity and makes it flow, impeding stratification. An equilibrium that is always re-establishing its own balance – inherent in the Mesoamerican concept of a universe in movement – also kept all other points of balance equally in constant motion. In a similar way, the categories of feminine and masculine were open and changing, as Lopez Austin seems to suggest: '. . . there was not a being exclusively feminine or exclusively masculine, but rather different nuances of combinations'.

II. Bodily and cosmic stability

The collective responsibility of not only sustaining balance but also participating in its achievement produced a very particular set of moral codes. The best expression of these moral codes is found in the discourses by the elders, the *huehuetlatolli* and *ilamatlatolli*.[7] As mentioned above, many Mexicanists regard Book VI of the *Florentine Codex* of Sahagún as a sort of *summa* of Nahuatl thought. It is the work which probes most deeply into the beliefs and norms of this society. The *ilamatlatolli* contained in Book VI of the *Florentine Codex* are explicitly about the type of equilibrium required in the conduct of women and men.

> . . . [D]o not walk hurriedly nor slowly . . . because walking slowly is a sign of pompousness and walking quickly shows restlessness and little sense. Walk moderately . . . Do not walk with your head lowered or your body slouched, but also do not carry your head overly high and upright because this is a sign of bad upbringing.[8]

... [Y]our garments (should) be modest, suitable. Do not dress strangely, nor extravagantly, nor eccentrically . . . Nor is it appropriate that your garments be ugly, dirty or torn . . .[9]

When you speak, do not speak rapidly . . . do not raise your voice nor speak too softly. . . Don't use a thin, high voice in speaking and greeting others, do not speak through your nose, but let your voice be normal.[10]

In the *huehuetlatolli*, we can appreciate balance as a constant of Nahuatl thought as it is incarnated in daily life, in relations between the genders, and in bodily attitudes. The body's immersion in the cosmos, and the insertion of the cosmos in the body doesn't allow even the possibility of a body/mind split.

1. The Mesoamerican body or permeable corporality

In dominant Western traditions, the very concept of body has been formed in opposition to mind. It is defined as the place of biological data, of the material, of the immanent. It has also been conceptualized since the seventeenth century as that which marks the boundaries between the interior self and the external world.

In the Mesoamerican tradition, on the other hand, the body has characteristics that are very different from those of the anatomical or biological body. Most notably, exterior and interior are not separated by the hermetic barrier of the skin. Between the outside and the inside, permanent and continuous exchange occurs. Material and immaterial, external and internal are in permanent interaction while the skin is constantly crossed by all kinds of entities. Everything leads towards a concept of corporality in which the body is open to all directions of the cosmos: a body, both single and dual, that incorporates solids and fluids in permanent flux, immaterial 'airs' or volatile emanations as well as 'juices' and solid matter. The Mesoamerican body can be imagined as a vortex generated by the dynamic confluence of multiple entities, both material and immaterial and often contradictory, that combine and recombine in an endless play.

2. Plurality of entities

In addition to the visible body, the Mesoamerican body is made up of "animic entities", as Lopez Austin calls them.[11] There are three pre-eminent animic entities: the *tonalli*, the *teyolia* and the *ihiyotl*. Each has its privileged

– but not unique – location within the physical body. The *tonalli*, whose principal residence is the head, travels at night during sleep. The *teyolia* resides in the heart and was regarded as the centre of memory, knowledge and intelligence. When the *teyolia* leaves the body, death occurs. The *ihiyotl* (breath or 'soplo'), which is associated with the liver, can produce emanations that harm others. The *ihiyotl* was the vital centre of passion and feeling. It is as part of this play of multiple emanations and inclusions that the body is conceptualized in Mesoamerican thought.[12]

3. The Nahua mode of being in the world

The world, for the Nahuas, was not 'out there', established outside of and apart from them. It was within them and even 'through' them. Actions and their circumstances were much more imbricated than is the case in Western thought where the 'I' can be analytically abstracted from its surroundings. Further, the body's porosity reflects an essential porosity of the cosmos, a permeability of the entire 'material' world that defines an order of existence characterized by continuous transit between the material and the immaterial. The cosmos emerges literally, in this conceptualization, as the complement of a permeable corporality. Klor de Alva writes:

> ... the Nahuas imagined their multidimensional being as an integral part of their body and of the physical and spiritual world around them.[13]

Besides, the 'conceptual being' of the Nahua was much less limited than that of Christians at the time of the Conquest and more inclined toward forming 'a physical and conceptual continuum with others, with the body and with the world beyond it . . .'[14]

4. Metaphors for the flesh

Metaphors make up the very fabric of Mesoamerican religious thought. Abundant and richly complex, metaphoric language was used in all aspects of life. Metaphors for the feminine and masculine body are found in the *ilamatlatolli* and *huehuetlatolli* (discourses of wise old women and men) from Book VI of *General History of the Things of New Spain*. Replete with metaphors, these discourses vividly illustrate specific cultural attitudes towards the bodies of women and men. As several researchers have pointed out, the discourses, recited publicly when children became adolescents, contain metaphors that give expression to fundamental components of Mesoamerican religious thought and morals as in the following examples:

... [F]rom the time of the lord of Tetzcuco, named Netzahualcoyotzin ... who asked them [two older women], saying: 'Grandmothers, tell me, is it true that you have desire for fleshly pleasure ... old as you are?'

The old women replied with a long explanation ending in a metaphor:

... [Y]ou men when you become old no longer desire carnal delights ... but we women never tire of these doings nor do we get enough of them because our bodies are like a deep abyss, a chasm that never fills up; it receives everything ... desiring more and asking for more ....[15]

In Book XVIII, there is the following advice for daughters:

Look now, don't choose from among the men the one that seems the best to you like those who shop for mantas in the market ... and don't carry on like people do when the new corn is just fresh, looking for the best and tastiest cobs ....[16]

Such metaphors about the bodies of women and men reveal aspects of the culture that were selectively eliminated by the first chroniclers and missionaries because they clashed with their own moral values. However, the metaphors surviving in everyday language probably seemed innocent enough and passed for mere poetic adornment of language. Sahagún would qualify them as 'very delicate and exact and adequate'. Metaphor carries the imprint of a culture's values. For example, socially accepted desire for the body of another is evident in the use of the metaphor 'the best and tastiest cobs'. It is evident likewise in the image of women's bodies as 'a deep abyss, a chasm that never fills up'.

These metaphors give us an idea of the bodily pleasures accepted in the Mesoamerican world. *Tlalticpacayotl*, translated as carnality or sex, literally means 'that which pertains to the surface of the earth'.[17] As with all that pertains to the earth's surface, erotic pleasure is earthly identity. Not only is it accepted, but it defines the inhabitants of Mesoamerica as dwellers of the four intermediate levels of the earth's surface. This abode of women and men is the place of the flesh, its joys and concerns. The earth would be inconceivable without the corporeal dimension.[18] To speak cosmically of eroticism is to speak of the dimensions belonging to 'the surface of the earth' and its central position in the Nahua cosmos.

III. Narrative and metaphor: Nahua corporality in the Florentine Codex

The narrative of the Tohuenyo or the Foreigner is a choice example for understanding body and gender in Nahua thought. Found in Book III of the *Florentine Codex*, it forms part of the wealth of documentation in Nahuatl about sixteenth-century Mexican culture collected by Sahagún and his assistants from indigenous informants in Tepepulco (Tezcoco region), Tlatelolco and Mexico beginning in 1547. The 'normative discourses' of the *huehuetlatolli* and *ilamataltolli* cannot be understood without narratives such as this, in which the cosmic meaning of pleasure becomes manifest. The story, part of epic narratives concerning divinities, is surprising for its bodily images and metaphors, as well as for the prominent place given to desire and carnality as expressed by a young girl. León-Portilla comments:

> It has been said at times concerning our indigenous culture that there is a lack of erotic themes (. . .) But, contrary to those who think this way, there are some old texts in Nahuatl, collected from native lips at the time of the conquest.[19]

This text was probably one of 'those old Nahuatl "texts" with a certain rhythm and measure that was learned by heart in the *calmecac* or other Nahua centres of superior education . . .'[20] Nahuatl youth in these centres received intellectual training as they listened to the *tlamatinime* (the wise men, or philosophers) express the highest values of their culture. It was also a place of training for the priesthood. '. . . [T]here is no doubt that the teachings directed at the most select of Nahuatl youth included the highest thinking, often contained in the songs and discourses learned by memory.'[21]

The story of the Tohuenyo concerns the erotic ardor that, without hyperbole, overcame a Toltec princess.[22] Here then, in León-Portilla's recent translation, is an excerpt from the story of the Tohuenyo.

> He went about naked, his thing just hanging,
> he began selling chilies,
> setting up his stand in the market, in front of the palace . . .
> So then that daughter of Huemac
> looked toward the market
> and saw the Tohuenyo: there with his thing hanging.
> As soon as she saw him,
> she went into the palace.

> Then, because of this, the daughter of Huemac fell sick.
> She became filled with tension, she entered into great heat,
> feeling herself deprived of the Tohuenyo's bird – his manly part – . . .
> 'That's how it began, that's how it is that she fell sick.'
> And the lord Huemac, seeing this, gave orders and said,
> 'Toltecs, look for the chili vendor,
> find the Tohuenyo.'
> And immediately they went about looking for him everywhere . . .
> But a little later Tohuenyo appeared on his own . . .
> Then the lord said to him:
> 'You have awakened that yearning in my daughter,
> You will cure her.' . . .
> And right away they cut his hair,
> they bathed him and after this
> they rubbed him with oils,
> put a loincloth on him and tied on a cloak.
> And when Tohuenyo went to see her,
> he immediately stayed with her
> and with this she got well that moment.[23]

Tohuenyo later won the recognition of the Toltecs and led them to victory in many battles. The story of his extraordinary war deeds became part of an epic myth about the adventures of supernatural beings of whom Tohuenyo is one. In the middle of these heroic deeds comes this 'remarkable story of the Tohuenyo', as León-Portilla calls it. It still surprises us that, despite the moral scrutiny and expurgation that the vestiges of erotic Nahua art suffered at the hands of the clerical chroniclers, this has survived.[24]

To find a text with an explicitly carnal content leads us to another level of understanding about the role of the body and desire in Nahuatl thought and culture. These expressions are very far from any sort of fear of the power of feminine desire, or from the fear of inexhaustible sexuality as found in Europe in the *Malleus Maleficarum*, for instance.[25]

Generally, historians emphasize the disciplined and to a certain degree repressive (as we would say) character of Aztec culture. Without a doubt, there were norms with respect to sex. At the same time, we cannot simplistically declare that no space existed for eroticism. In a culture and thought produced by duality, by the alternating presence of opposites in motion, the demands of discipline were enriched by the possibility of and esteem for carnality. The one-sided emphasis on rigour and discipline is more a product of the values of the missionary historians than a true reflection of the data and realities of that ancient world. What Sahagún recorded in Chapter VII, Book VI of the *General History of the Things of New Spain* balances the picture:

> ... They worshipped Tlazulteotl, the deity of lust, the Mexicas did, especially the Mixtecs and Olmecs ... and the Cueztecs worshipped and honored Tlazulteotl, and didn't accuse themselves of lust before him, because for them lust was not a sin.

Conclusion

In revisiting these ancient Mesoamerican body concepts and percepts, it is appropriate to stress that women's bodies are not only recognized and venerated for their reproductive capacity, but that they are also subjects of desire. The body, abode and axis of delights and pleasures, the dual body of women and men, fluid and permeable corporality, is the principle of being on earth, in fusion with the immediate surrounding and with the origin of the cosmos. Glimpses of this feminine and masculine and cosmic body can be caught in remnants of epic poetry, songs, narratives, and metaphors. Even these vestiges can begin to reveal incarnate universes that escape the Western master narrative of spirit over flesh.

Notes

(All translations of primary sources in Spanish are by the author.)

1. Fray Bernardino de Sahagún, *Historia general de las cosas de Nueva España* (first integral Spanish version of the Nahuatl manuscript known as *Florentine Codex*), edited by Alfredo Lopez Austin and Josefina Garcia Quitana, Mexico: Consejo Nacional para la Cultura y las Artes and Alianza Editorial Mexicana, 1989, 2 vols.

    With the help of a questionnaire that Fray Bernardino de Sahagún elaborated in his search for relevant information about the Nahuatl world, his assistants collected material in Nahuatl. This original material can be found in the *Royal Palace Matritense Codex*, which is the Nahuatl source that León-Portilla uses for his new translations. (I consulted the version edited by Francisco del Paso y Troncoso, *Codice Matritense del Real Palacio*, Vol. VII, phototype by Hauser and Menet, Madrid 1906.)

    The *Royal Palace Matritense Codex* is thus the collection in Nahuatl by Sahagún and his assistants of the material they gathered from informants. For a discussion of the origin of Sahagún's work and the complexities of dealing

with the sources, see Sylvia Marcos, 'Gender and Moral Precepts in Ancient Mexico: Sahagún's Texts', *Concilium*, December 1991.
2. Andrés de Olmos, 'Historia de los Mexicanos por sus pinturas', in A. Garibay, (ed.), *Teogonia e Historia de los Mexicanos. Tres opúsculos del siglo XVI*, Mexico: Porrua 1973.
3. Yolotl Gonzales Torres, *Diccionario de Mitología y Religión de Mesoamérica*, Mexico: Larousse 1991, p. 125: '. . . 4 (referred to) the four directions of the universe, 5 (to) the four directions plus the center, 9 was associated with the underworld and 13 (referred to) the levels of heaven, the underworld and earth plus the center'.
4. Alfredo Lopez Austin, 'Cosmovisión y Salud entre los Méxicas', in Alfredo Lopez Austin and Carlos Viesca (eds), *Historia de la Medicina en México*, Book I. Mexico: UNAM, Facultad de Medicina 1984, p. 103.
5. Jacques Soustelle, *La Pensée Cosmologique des Anciens Mexicains*, Paris: Herman et Cie 1955.
6. For a discussion of Greek thought in relation to Nahuatl modes of thought, see Sylvia Marcos, 'Categorías de género y pensamiento mesoamericano: un reto epistemológico', in *La Palabra y el Hombre*, Jalapa, Veracruz: Universidad Veracruzana, October 1995.
7. For an extensive treatment of the *huehuetlatolli* and *ilamatlatolli* in relation to gender in Mesoamerica, see Sylvia Marcos, 'Gender and Moral Precepts in Ancient Mexico: Sahagún's texts', *Concilium*, December 1991.
8. Sahagún, *Historia general* (n.1), Book VI, p. 371.
9. Ibid., p. 384.
10. Ibid., p. 383.
11. Lopez Austin, 'Cosmovisión y Salud entre los Méxicas' (n.4).
12. Rémi Siméon, *Diccionario de la lengua nahuatl o mexicana*, Mexico: Siglo Veintiuno 1988 (original: *Dictionnaire de la Langue Nahuatl ou Mexicaine*, 1885).
13. Jorge Klor de Alva, , 'Contar vidas: la autobiografía confesional y la reconstrucción del ser nahua', in *Arbor*, No. 515–16, Madrid 1988, pp. 49–78.
14. Ibid.
15. Sahagún, *Florentine Codex* (n.1), p. 382.
16. Ibid., p. 369.
17. Alfredo Lopez Austin, 'Cosmovisión y Salud entre los Méxicas' (n.4).
18. Perhaps this was the reason why ancient Mesoamericans regarded the negation of carnal activities as abnormal since without them, one didn't belong to the earth.
19. Miguel León-Portilla, see below, n.23.
20. Ibid.
21. Miguel León-Portilla, *Aztec Thought and Culture*, Norman and London: University of Oklahoma Press 1990.

22. Angel M. Garibay, *Historia de la literatura nahuatl*, Mexico: Porrua 1953. The original Nahuatl narrative transcribed by Sahagún can be found in Francisco del Paso y Troncoso, *Codice Matritense del Real Palacio* (n.1).
23. The new translation from Nahuatl into Spanish is from Miguel León-Portilla, *Toltecayotl, Aspectos de la Cultura Nahuatl*, Mexico: Fondo de Cultura Económica 1980. The English translation is by the author.
24. Sahagún's translation of this Nahuatl narrative into Spanish is from Book III of his *Historia general de las cosas de la Nueva España* [1577]. However, more than a translation, it is is a summary of the narrative in which the adjectives and metaphors are toned down, even altered. Noting the changes this poetic story underwent at the hands of Sahagún allows us to suppose that other texts by other missionary chroniclers with bodily and erotic implications underwent similar alterations. Yet, Sahagún was much more respectful than others in conserving, albeit modified, the teachings and discourses that did not agree with his moral values. The changes made by Sahagún and other chroniclers were subject to the evangelizing purpose of their writings, the pressure exerted by the Inquisition, and the shame or reserve the monks could have experienced when faced with certain Mesoamerican expressions of desire and pleasure.
25. *Malleus Maleficarum*, in Latin, by Heinrich Kramer and James Sprenger, both Dominicans, appeared in 1484 (or 1486 according to other authors). From this sadly renowned document, written to help hunt 'witches' and later condemn them to the Inquisition's fire, comes the idea of women envious of masculine genitals, insatiable, and thus dangerous for men. The work almost seems to imply that all men are near saints and that only the evil influence of women keeps them from dedicating their lives to the service or God or to the elevated (bodiless) activities of the mind.

Embodiment and Connexity: An African Purview

GOSBERT T. M. BYAMUNGU

Introduction

Disasters are a good occasion for growth. Indeed, recent international events have prompted a change of stress in this article. Documentations on the HIV/AIDS Day on 1 December 2001 substantially affected my reflections on the human body. Notwithstanding the propensity to exaggeration, the world focus was on Africa and the statistics shocking. A significant portion of the human race is being wiped out every day.[1] Affected, I had to go back to the paper and think differently on the subject. Although sexual promiscuity is not the only way through which HIV/AIDS is transmitted, it is easily the most prevalent. This struck a chord of responsibility in me, so that I asked: 'How can we break the patterns so as to create a healthier world?'

This renders the thrust of my paper a complicated affair. The decision to look at the most crucial aspects regarding the assault on the human body in the contemporary African situation left my analysis ramified into three: the relational, the sexual and the pragmatical. The latter looks at the body and its limitation by disease and death.

I. The body and connexity

1. Contact between mother and child

There is a direct contact between the body of the unborn child and the mother's womb. In Africa, this contact continues after birth through breast feeding and childcare: The mother, sister or brother carry the baby on the back. There is intimacy, security, connection, solidarity. This intimate touch between bodies is tremendously therapeutic. It has power potential as well: whoever is elder commands respect for his or her contribution.

That uncovers an important aspect of the concept of embodiment in African cultural purview: connexity. A mother will seldom untie the baby from her back as she jumps to the sound of the drums. The art and the joys are transmitted from mother even to the unborn child, by participation. That is why African children never have formal training for the dance, and that is why Africans are joyous by nature. The culture is intrinsic to all Africans across the globe, and the music and the dance are integral to all rituals from birth to death. In all this the body is protagonist.

In all these joyous events, sexual identity is central. Men dance in pairs with women where the dance requires two. Indeed, in many ethnic groups people dance moving the lower parts of their bodies, which can be sexually provocative. However, the people who do it don't always mean to be provacative, as the offertory dance during worship among the Baganda proves. The girls who take the gifts of the worshipping community to the altar dance moving the lower parts of their bodies in praise and honour to God. Their movements, although they can be interpreted sexually, are not intended to be erotic. One relates to God as to a human person holistically as it were, body and soul. It is for this reason that worship in Africa involves the significant participation of the body.

2. *The ontology of embodiment*

To an African, the human body is metaphysically conceived as an organic unit of relating. An individual exists in a world of relationships inside which one occupies an important place. My being is expressible in terms of how I relate to phenomena around me prior to my being and with consequences to my actual relating. I am alive in the world thanks to a network of relationships. The Yagba People of the Gambia in West Africa prospectively link this ontology to embodiment. They call the body *ara*, which means 'that through which a person attracts favour'. It is through the *ara* that one achieves connection to one's environment.[2]

To happen favourably, connection depends on the impression one makes on others. The Bahaya of North-Western Tanzania have linguistic expressions that can help to understand this ontology. There is the same semantical enunciation to contradistinguish between 'wrong', 'evil', 'bad', and 'ugly', composed of the suffix *-ub'i*. 'Evil' is *b-ubi*, to do 'wrong' is *kukora* (to do) *k-ubi*; to be a 'bad guy' is *kuba* (to be) *m-ubi*; to be 'ugly' is *kuba* (to be) *m-ubi*. A disagreeable person is designated as *muntu m-ubi*, which means both an 'evil' and 'ugly' one. The precise linguistic nuance that puts evil and ugliness on an equal footing argues for an ontological space in which what is intrinsically an interior disposition (evil) is also (*double entendre*) physically expressible as ugliness. The metaphysical concept of evil is expressible also physically as 'ugly'. One manifests one's ontological configuration through one's bodily impression into the world.

Indeed, metaphysics spews out morality, social politics, and relational anthropology. This metaphysical conception of 'evil/bad/ugly' is complimented by its antonym concept of 'good/beautiful'. A young man aspiring to a married status among the Bahaya needs to be a *musigazi murungi*, meaning 'good/comely', both as a moral and physical constitution, put together. A *musigazi murungi* is not simply one 'pleasant to look at', but also one with good moral reputation. The all-important suffixed term *-urungi* is the opposite of *-ubi* (analysed above), and it means anything relating to goodness (internal constitution) and comeliness (external configuration). To be good inside, one needs to be goodly on the outside.

II. The sexual power of the body

Among the Kpelle, one of the largest tribes in Liberia and Guinea, the word 'body' is signified by *kponoo*, and is nuanced as 'that through which one is linked to the others'. *Kponoo* also means 'exposure of the sexual organ(s)'.[3] For the Kpelle, the concept of the human body embraces sexual identity. In the same way, the term to denote 'body' among the Efik of South-Eastern Nigeria is *idem*, which also means genital organs. Evidence exists from diverse African ethnic groups to show how the concept of body is culturally associated with sexuality.

The Bahaya manifest love publicly during the 'send-off party'. On this day, the groom takes the final part of the 'dowry'; he will be officially recognized and traditionally married before the Christian wedding takes place on the following day. Part of the ceremony is to make an 'epiphany' of the 'man who is to marry our daughter', and the 'woman who has won the love of our son'. Two families will merge into one and will sit together to celebrate the new union. The peers of the groom and those of the bride will perform a public showing of the couple amidst singing and dancing. The friends bring the groom and the bride in turns. Both are covered with a mantle, and they will be exposed at the opportune moment during the performance. The dance stops when the moment comes, the mantle is lifted, and the groom or the bride's face (as the turn may be), is uncovered. People will then shout with joy to the beauty, the comely features of the man/woman who has won the love of their daughter/son. The stress is on the bodily features in public manifestation.

Across the continent, what takes place among the Bahaya of Tanzania happens among the Efik of Nigeria. Their basic philosophy on the matter is contained in the expression: '*ikpok idem emi abasi onode mi ntetim nkama*', which means, 'this body (*idem*) given to me by God, I must take good care of it'. Among the Efik, shortly before marriage, the bride is always put in a room (*ufok nkuho*), where her body is prepared to meet the man of her life. It is treated to make it supple before she goes out for the wedding. Part of this treatment is to feed her with good food, so that she might have good looks as she meets her husband.[4] The point is to attract, which is an important ingredient for the stable love relationship that is about to begin. Here eroticism is celebrated for its affectiveness. The aim is to safeguard marriage. Such elements on sexuality were later discarded as pagan.

1. Christianity and sin

The negative judgment on sex came with Christianity. The Fathers of the church, drawing from Plato, considered the human person as a quasi-political entity within which the soul struggled against the body. In the *City of God*, Augustine envisions a world order in harmonious obedience to God. This order is upset because a tiny prohibition becomes a cause of disobedience.[5] From that moment, things could never be the same again: Man could no longer master himself.[6] Following Paul in Romans 7, Augustine in *De Nuptiis et Concupiscentia* comes down to the point: Man can master every member of his body, except his lust for sexual pleasure.[7] Augustine deals with men's problems and dwells at length with how lust takes control from man, making sexual activity and the sexual organs shameful.[8] He proceeds to pair this problem of sexual desire with that of sexual pleasure. For him this is disturbing:

> . . . it disturbs the whole man, the mental emotion being joined to and mixed with the fleshly appetite, so that a pleasure follows greater than all bodily pleasures. It is such that at the moment when it reaches its climax almost all awareness and as it were the guards of thought are overwhelmed. Which friend of wisdom and of holy joys, living a married life . . . would not prefer, if he could, to beget children without this lust?[9]

I may sound anachronistic, but Augustine could not be farther from what the evidence shows to be true: instead of desiring to have children without orgasm as Augustine desires it, people will desire orgasm without children. Because of this propensity to separate sexual pleasure from procreation, fear that people might involve in sexual activities for the sake of pleasure alone became a grave moral preoccupation. It became so suspect and so wrong for Augustine and for later tradition that it became sin.[10]

In Africa, this attribution of sin to sex became a fixation and infiltrated the whole culture. This dichotomy affected life in Africa, and I cite again the Bahaya as an example. The researcher R. Albrecht observes that among the Bahaya Christians, 'sin' occupied 21% of sermons. This compares unevenly with other topics like 'God's work of creation' (10%), 'various attributes of God' (10%), 'God's love and Grace' (15%) and God's presence through 'new means' (18%).[11] Although statistics can be bent to suit a perspective, the point he makes is clear. 'Sin' became such a preoccupation that it hampered life. Interestingly, the words *bufu* and *ntambara* which denote 'sin' among the Bahaya belong to a semantical cluster which is different from the *-ubi* suffix we have analysed above, meaning 'evil/bad/ugly'. *Bufu* and *ntambara* refer respectively to natural and to promulgated law. While *bufu* implies an idea of permissiveness, of lethal carelessness, *ntambara* stresses the aspect of transgressing a penal code. While *bufu* leads to a possible death, *ntambara* leads to a punishment. In Christianity, this distinction disappeared and both were fused into moral law. The bigger problem was the identification of 'sex' with 'sin', and Christian sanctity came to be measured only by the sixth commandment. Thus the sexual organs are euphemistically called *ebibi*, literally, the 'evil/bad/ugly' things!

This pairing of 'evil/ugly' with sexual organs derives from the traditional 'Christian' association of sex with evil/sin. The link adversely affected healthy sexual relationships in such a way that what is actually experienced as pleasurable and attractive is paradoxically prohibited by religion as evil and ugly. This creates unnecessary tension between will and duty, and adversely affects religion and religious people. People refrain from healthy relationships and engage in promiscuous sex in secret so as to 'steal' a pleasurable moment under cover as the occasion arises. Unwittingly, by forbidding 'the fruit' one makes it more attractive.

Friedrich Nietzsche put it succinctly: 'Christianity gave Eros poison to drink – he didn't die from it, but he did degenerate, into a vice.'[12] What Nietzsche is saying is that the condemnation of erotic pleasure does not succeed in making people refrain from its pursuit. Rather, it succeeds only in making them pursue it with a sense of guilt. This seems to be the empirical evidence world-wide.

2. Christianity and friendship

It is possible that the problems facing Africa in respect of HIV/AIDS arise from this tension. If people were encouraged to talk, learn, and assert the power of sexuality honestly, openly and positively, some of these problems could be considerably reduced. In Africa, the church offers sexual instruction to couples that are about to marry. In my view the instruction comes too late!

My proposal is to look at sexual pleasure a little more closely. Doing pleasurable things just because they are pleasurable is an ordinary human good. I like to spend hours in meditation because it is immeasurably pleasant. People play or watch football, arrange meals together, share a drink, just because the experience is pleasurable. So is reading a book, listening to music, or going to movies. No one is expected to justify one's pleasure in these activities. The only pleasure that has to be justified by childbearing is sexual pleasure.

Far from being a threat to Christian living, the desire of sex for the pleasure it gives can be used as a basis for a healthy Christian sexual ethic that embodies recognizably Christian values which also accommodate traditional Christian attitudes to sex. Christians have always maintained that the proper place for sex is within the context of a relation of friendship, whose ultimate mode is marriage. This allows the assertion that rather than being its enemy, sexual pleasure is the friend of Christian thought. Put differently, Christianity does not seek to limit pleasure as it were, but tries to enhance and protect it as a Christian ethic, so that to have sexual pleasure one needs to do so with a person one delights in. This is why Christianity has always blessed marriage.

III. The limits of the body

The body, which can be attractive, can also be delicate, easily troubled by disease and annihilated by death. Medicine, which protects it, is said to be more art than science.[13] Indeed, a German physician who worked for many years in my country confided to me his perplexities about many patients who found it difficult to locate pains in their bodies. His explanation was that the culture did not allow enough human touching, an essential element in health care.

My concern is with Africa. Africa harbours a colonial vice, which is never to think about its own problems without quoting philosophies and/or theologies from abroad. The battle which stares Africa in the face challenges

African theologians and church men and women to think and act contextually.

1. Diversifying bodily pleasure

Our context is that of a continent beset with immense problems. Africa cannot afford to lose its labour power through death seminated through sex. Is sex the only field where bodily energies can be spent? An array of activities in which people can find pleasure is available. Aristotle admonishes that pleasure consists in *doing* things.[14] Africa needs to do many things, and energies can be spent on doing them. African relational metaphysics can be amplified to include the whole of creation: plants, animals and people. People can create gardens, build roads, schools, health centres, for the sheer pleasure of becoming co-creators with God. All these activities involve the body, and one can discover an immense pleasure in just doing them. Africans excel in sports and in music. These activities can be promoted for reasons of health.

2. Healthy sexual pleasure

There is still more to be said. Africans have a deep sense of shame over sex. Parents will hardly discuss sex with their children. Euphemistic discourse about sexual organs reveals that they are a private zone (*sehemu za siri*), secrets behind clothing (*siri za nguoni*). What is private may not be discussed in public. Yet, there was a certain framework of discretion in which parents gave their children an essential sexual education before marriage. Customary laws protected unmarried women from abuse, and sex was safeguarded within a marriage contract. This is why marriage was liberal: monogamous, polygamous, polyandric. It was to safeguard relationships. This was complicated by Christianity, urbanization and pluralism.

The problem was and still is that a woman is never married to an individual but to a family, indeed, to a clan (*ushemeji*). The aim was to increase the clan regardless of how men and women within the same clan mixed sexually. Promiscuity through *ushemeji* remains common, even among Christians. Black African society has to be honest and rethink these mixed ethics to meet contemporary challenges. The original culture of intimacy in which people received and offered pleasure in different bodily contacts such as embraces, strokes, looks, plays, or simply being together to celebrate an event, drink and eat together in mixed company need to be enhanced as a variety of legitimate interaction.

In interpersonal relationships, pleasure is much wider than excitement and it consists in doing things together within a shared space. To seek casual pleasures for the excitement they may give deprives the person of the fulfillment pleasure is capable of giving. This is what makes casual sex with strangers defective, and argues against promiscuity, clearly an enemy of the body, especially in Africa.

We need to understand that it is not the intention of Christianity to put a curb on sexual pleasure, but only to honour and safeguard it. Christianity's methods need to be re-examined, so that legitimate pleasures can be set free. My dream would be to see the church and the state co-operating to educate people. Power games must give way to the need to protect life. School and seminary syllabuses need to include sex education, so that children can learn about their bodies in a favourable light, and teachers must be equipped to help them competently.

3. The body and death

Among Africans, death is not the end of life, but a transition to another life with the ancestors in the land of the spirits. The one who will be remembered as an ancestor is the person who has lived as a 'good' one. So the Kpelle will wash the dead body properly, rub it with oil, and place it under a tent where appointed elders will stay with it until time comes for ceremonial burial. The details may differ, but the ceremony is identical across Africa. The Bahaya grandchildren will beat drums and enact the high points of the life of the deceased grandpa/grandma. Drums are not used in the burial of young people.

Conclusion

Africans value the human body, celebrate beauty and life. They take embodiment to be a medium of relationships, without which one cannot assert oneself in the world. In this connection, the body is essentially sexual, because it is only through sexually identified relationships that human beings come to be, relate and prolong life. This tradition is under threat, so it is important to face the challenge squarely. One way is to promote sex education and to revisit indigenous praxes to foster healthy relationships. A harmonious relationship between erotic pleasure and Christian morality is necessary so that God's creation can serve life.

Notes

1. It is said that about 28.1 million people are HIV/AIDS positive in Africa, and that this constitutes about 70% of the world total. In some countries, notably South Africa, it is said that about one out every three people are infected. The affected are mostly the élite, those most able to carry out the revolution Africa badly needs. The situation gravely affects the political, economic and social future of Africa.
2. My thanks go to Osaloto Daniel Sesin for this point.
3. I take these points from Thomas Zenah Paye (Kpelle)'s unpublished exposition, 'Traditional Kpelle Understanding of the Body'.
4. Acknowledgment goes to Prince Eyo Ubong Ekpenyong for his unpublished reflections 'The View of Human Body Among the Efik'.
5. *City of God* 14.12
6. *City of God* 12.24.
7. Cf. *De Nuptiis et Concupiscentia*, 1.6.
8. *City of God* 14.19: 'Lust has in a sense taken the genital parts of the body as its own property, so that they have no strength to move if lust is absent, and if it has not arisen spontaneously or through some stimulus. It is this that causes shame.'
9. *City of God* 14.16
10. Cf. Gareth Moore OP, *The Body in Context: Sex and Catholicism*, London and New York: Continuum 2001, pp. 47f..
11. Cf. R. Albrecht, 'Profile Through Presence: God in Contemporary Haya Sermons', in *African Theological Journal* 4, August 1971, pp. 40–55.
12. Friedrich Nietzsche, *Jenseits von Gut und Böse* (Beyond Good and Evil), no. 168 in *Sämtliche Werke: Kritische Studienausgabe* ed. Giorgio Colli and Mazzino Montinari, vol. 5, 2nd edn Munich: DTV and Berlin and New York: de Gruyter 1988, p. 102.
13. Cf. Dalia Judovitz, *The Culture of the Body: Genealogies of Modernity*, Ann Arbor: The University of Michigan Press 2001, p. 21.
14. *Nichomachean Ethics* 10.4.1–10.5.5.

Suffering, Resisting, Healing: An Asian View of the Body

SHARON A. BONG

A theology that matters is one that is embodied. That Asian Christian theology is 'body language, heart semantics or soul-syntax' reclaims the body and its corporeality in theologizing from the lived experiences of the grassroots and in particular, women.[1] It is premised on the historical and material conditions of specific Asian communities and articulated from their positions of marginality *and* agency. And it effects the following doctrinal transgressions. It is firstly an antithesis to the denigration of the body fed by the church's tacit valorization of asceticism and residual misogyny of the (male) spirit/(female) body duality. Secondly, it digests the humanization of God in the body of Christ that suffers, resists and heals and in so doing, eschews a Godhead that is disembodied. And thirdly, it rejects the exegetic 'violence of abstraction'[2] by foregrounding faith and praxis towards the realization of a local/global community that is more equitable, just and sustainable from within the church and beyond.

In contrast, from my personal standpoint as an Asian-Malaysian Catholic feminist, the platter of doctrinal interpretation of the 'economy of "signs"' served on women's bodies, sexuality and roles has become not only unsavoury but also distasteful.[3] Women are equal but different within the equation of the complementarity of the sexes. Secondly, women are divested of the capacity to act '*in persona Christi*' (imaging Christ) notwithstanding their 'feminine genius'. This essential lack inherent in the ontology of women, her very being, affords the irrefutable and therefore irreversible rationale to women's exclusion from priestly ordination.[4] And thirdly, extolling the virtue of 'heroic love' of women who refuse to abort a foetus resulting from 'the injustice of rape'[5] evinces the 'violence of abstraction' of a theology disconnected from the signs of the times. Its maturity date for those who inhabit and negotiate their bodies and sexualities within the intersection of gender, race, caste, class, cultures and religions, has long expired.

Suffering, Resisting, Healing

Bodies that suffer, bodies that resist and bodies that heal constitute the life-blood, sinew and fibre of Christian theologies from Asia. In this article, with 'an economy' of words, I reflect on the centrality and limits of theologizing on the materiality of bodies that are pathologized (bodies that suffer), politicized (bodies that resist) and spiritualized (bodies that heal).

I. Bodies that suffer

Imaging a suffering Christ is literalized in women (and men) who are dehumanized. An embodied theology in faithful allegiance to Christ's preferential option and actualization of scarred bodies confers hermeneutical privilege on the biblical poor. It does so in recognition of the lived realities of Asian women (and men) who are pinioned by structural and systemic violence in the form of gender, racial, caste, class, cultural and religious oppressions.

The bodies that suffer are thus those who know (suffering) as opposed to the primacy of historically laudable mediators of knowledge, translators of experience and codifiers of faith. And they are mothers, wives, daughters, sisters who are victims and survivors of familial violence in the form of female infanticide, incest, dowry deaths, honour killings, domestic violence (which includes marital rape); communal and military violence in the mass rape of women from ethnic minorities, outcast (i.e. Dalit of India) or indigenous communities; state violence manifest in rape, torture, summary executions and forced relocation, labour and deportation of women in situations of armed conflict; and global violence through the trafficking of women and girls and inhumane treatment of migrant and sex workers and disenfranchized sexual minorities. They are the 12,612 dowry deaths recorded across India in 1998-9 where new brides were starved, beaten, tortured, imprisoned at home and/or doused with paraffin and set alight by their husbands or mothers-in-law because their families failed to make 'adequate' dowry payments to the husband's family.[6]

It is women's bodies constructed as repositories and markers of ethnic, cultural and religious boundaries that result in women's greater vulnerability to racism, racial and ethnic discrimination, xenophobia and related intolerance which not only affect women in different ways and degrees from men but also exacerbate gender-based violence.[7] It is the 168 Indonesian women and girls of mostly Chinese descent who were gang raped in the streets and raped in front of their families during the mid-May 1998 Jakarta riots.[8]

It is the appropriation of women's bodies as a site of contestation between fundamentalism and feminism: where women's bodies in the former ideology serve as retainers of pristine and immutable identity and in the latter, as breeding ground for polluting subversive change. The scene is the 1994 Cairo International Conference on Population and Development (ICPD); the script, 'replete with death threats from militant Egyptian Muslim groups, eschatological rhetoric from the Vatican' amid the dissonant chorus of women's health, rights and empowerment; and the 'prop', women's bodies, their sexuality and their roles in family and society.[9]

It is the inscription of women's bodies as a lesser body that is the foundational premise of son preference endemic in Asian cultures and contentiously, in the church. This predisposes a girl-child to a life of gender-based violence, in particular early marriage (including child marriage) and sexual exploitation and a life of deprivation in terms of adequate access to food, health, education and love. It is nearly one seventh of Chinese baby girls missing – for every 100 girls registered at birth, there are 118 little boys – as a result of female infanticide (or baby dumping) and prenatal sex selection (illegal, selective abortion) as extensions of son preference.[10]

The democratization of Asian theology reinstates the primacy of bodies that suffer into the body of the canon. Hermeneutical privilege is thus accorded to them and the 'community becomes the theologian'.[11] They thereby serve as the pulse of Asian theologies of liberation for they liberate theology from its doctrinal abstractions, hegemony and disconnectedness. To illustrate the centrality of the oppressed as the foundational basis of theologies from Asia, 'Dalit theology' or 'No people's theology' embraces the 'no-humanness' of *dalits* (pariah of Indian society) as symptomatic of the negation of their humanity, yet strives to realize their 'full divinity' as created in God's image (*Imago Dei*).[12] In so doing, theologies premised on bodies that suffer call for the 'primacy of anthropological element over the ecclesiastical', 'utopian over the factual', 'critical over the dogmatic', 'social over the personal' and 'orthopraxis over orthodoxy'.[13]

Theologizing from the vantage point of the marginalized does not detract from but essentially concretizes Christ's preferential option for the poor: where one's compassion and interconnectedness with those who are more dispirited is the hallmark of Two-Thirds world women and men *doing* theology. It stretches the limits of Christianity as an eschatological faith premised on the potential and obligation of human agency to evince a better tomorrow today: to approximate a heaven on earth. This conviction then materializes into a catalytic spirit that embraces solidarity with the marginalized and culminates in an 'eruption from below'.[14] In profoundly identifying with the poor, in being a servant to the poor, in conferring upon the poor the dignity of self-determination, theologians reinstate the plural and radical voice of the marginalized of Asia as the cornerstone of theologies of, for and by Asians.

However, eschewing an exegetic 'violence of abstraction' runs the risk of pathologizing bodies that suffer: of inscribing Asian bodies, particularly Asian women's bodies as weak, infirmed and violated. On one level, the inferiorization, subjugation and victimization of women and the girl-child from birth to grave substantiate bodies that suffer as knowing subjects of theological discourse as argued above. But hermeneutical and political privileging of bodies that suffer is also problematized. For instance, the 'theology of "the poor woman" in Asia' has its discursive limits as Wong Wai Ching deconstructs the monolithic categorization of 'the poor woman' as a metonym for human suffering. Within the economy of a nationalistic rhetoric and strategy that dichotomizes the colonized Asian against the Western imperialist, women's individuated historical and political agency is often subsumed. Women's bodies are on the one hand homogenously constructed as victimized to justify colonial intervention in the form of civilizing missions; on the other hand, they are propped up as barometers of national essence to preserve tradition and to fortify resistance. Within a postcolonial identity politics, she is thus doubly colonized: denigrated as 'poor woman' and idealized as 'superwoman'.[15]

II. Bodies that resist

Theologizing therefore begins with an awareness of the pitfalls of pathologizing and its attendant risks of romanticizing and appropriating the narratives of subjugated positions. It follows through with a conviction that foregrounding bodies that suffer as the foundational premise of theology would potentially illuminate the underlying causes of structural and systemic sin towards the realization of a transformative vision of the world. Solidarity with the oppressed and substantiation of our collective and reciprocal self-worth and determination thus serve as prerequisites to the authentication of embodied theologies from Asia.

As such, hermeneutical subjects or bodies that know are also bodies that resist. In breaking the silence on sexuality, they generate new ways of seeing which are grounded, specific and critical. It is those who challenge homophobia and heterosexism in negotiating sexuality from a human rights perspective:[16] whereby women – as affirmed in the *Beijing Platform For*

Action, the international blueprint of women's human rights – are 'to have control over and decide freely and responsibly on matters related to their sexuality, including sexual and reproductive health, free of coercion, discrimination and violence'.[17] It is those who recognize that empowering women does not disempower men in stemming the HIV/AIDS pandemic in Asia: that more gender-equitable relationships significantly reduce the risk of vulnerability of *both* women and men to HIV infection.[18] It is those who redefine virginity on their own terms in embracing chastity of mind, body and spirit and those who reject the construct of virginity as proof of a woman's marriageable worth.[19] It is those who demystify the regulation of women's sexuality and representation as 'ornamented surface' for the gratification of male pleasure and gaze.[20] And it is the 80 comfort women who broke the silence of their victimization in a mock tribunal on Japan's World War II enslavement of at least 200,000 women in military brothels in occupied territories in South East Asia and East Asia.[21]

It is the bodies that resist seamless categorizations within the plurality and proliferation of identities embroiled in multi-ethnic, multi-cultural and multi-religious contexts in Asia compounded by the disparity between the have and have-nots therein. It is the implausibility and indecency of ranking hierarchically suffering and resistant bodies. It is Vietnamese women opting for cosmetic surgery in pursuit of the idealization of Western standards of beauty to embellish their Asian features *and* Bangladeshi women who receive reconstructive surgery as survivors of acid attacks to refigure physical but not emotional scars.[22] It is not de-sexualizing the grassroots as bodies that suffer and bodies that resist in agitating for structural change within the church and society. It is avoiding the violent othering of the Other in embracing gay, lesbian, bisexual, trans-sexual, trans-gendered and other disinherited bodies as well as the single, widowed and childless as deviations from normative heterosexual and (re)-productive relations. It is recognizing that the bodies that do not have enough to eat, bodies that overeat and bodies that refuse to eat rest on the same continuum of need. It is coming to terms with the inequitable distribution of the world's resources that account for hunger and obesity as corollary eating disorders. And it is being aware that voluntary starvation is paradoxically a protest against the construction of women's bodies and regulation of women's sexualities as well as an eroticization of thinness as a beauty myth that is internally inflicted.

III. Bodies that heal

In 'an epistemology of the broken body', the restoration of bodies that suffer and bodies that resist becomes the dialectical site of redemption, for as Chung Hyun Kyung contends, 'to be human is to suffer and resist' and 'to be human is to be created in God's image'.[23] For Asians where the spirit is corporeal and the body (and sexuality) sacred, by inference, the body is the spirit. The configuration of the human person as both body *and* spirit reinstates not only their human agency but also human worth and in repositioning the spirit as corporeal and the body as sacred, Asian theologians depart from doctrinal eschatology that maintains the inferiorization of material and sexualized bodies.

The benchmark of Christianity in Asia is as such, its insistence on praxis – faith translated as compassionate identification and solidarity with the marginalized. The Asian sense of ecclesiastical mission as premised on the 'epistemology of the broken body' – alluding simultaneously to the crucifixion of Christ as/and bodies that suffer, resist and heal – attests to the concretization of a transformative faith that witnesses the transition from '*anthropocentrism to life-centrism*' and the adoption of 'voluntary [spiritual] poverty' in dialectical opposition to 'forced [material] poverty'.[24] Embodied theologies thus problematize dualisms such as mind/body, spirit/matter, abstract/concrete, objective/subjective, theory/praxis, universal/particular, observer/observed and male/female.

For Asian theologies, the representation of God in the anthropomorphic Christ is both transcendent *and* immanent. God therefore is not immutable and dispassionate but is embodied in and through the oppressed. The phenomenon of a '*christological transformation*' is exacted through the use of 'religio-political symbols' to encapsulate unique images of Christ concordant with the experiences of Asian peoples.[25] The postcolonial portrayal of Jesus as 'liberator, revolutionary and political martyr' mirrors the political martyrdom of Filipino women in their relentless crusade for social transformation: that they 'do not merely accompany Christ to Calvary as spectators [but also] carry the cross with him and undergo his passion in an act of identification with his suffering' and in so doing, resurrect 'the *Bagong Kristo* (the New Christ)' that resides within them.[26] Through a 'christology from below'[27] God is thus transmuted and humanized. Knowledge of God as omniscient, omnipresent and omnipotent is arbitrated through the agency of the suffering and resistant and God the Signifier thus becomes known, present and empowering.

An emerging Asian spirituality of, for and by Asian people is fundamentally a theology that necessitates the politics of difference and the politics of identity premised on the socially determinate lives of its knowing subjects – the bodies that suffer, resist and are healed. A theology that matters is a theology that is embodied. And a theology that is embodied is sound theology. The spirituality of Asian people affords a site of theological inquiry to the question of praxis or committed action. The politicization of spirituality and the spiritualization of politics endemic in Asian theologizing prophetically herald the eschatological promise of begetting a heaven on earth. It is the realization of an equitable, just and sustainable global/local community from within the church and beyond. It is in the context of Asia, ceasing to wonder at the extent to which favouring sons and neglecting daughters, is sanctioned by the 'economy of "signs"' of the body of the church.

Notes

1. C. S. Song quoted in Charles Elliott, *Sword and Spirit*, London 1989, p. 42.
2. Chung Hyun Kyung, *Struggle to be the Sun Again: Introducing Asian Women's Theology*, London and New York 1990, p. 101.
3. 'Pope John Paul II's Letter to Women' issued (10 July 1995) to address the Fourth United Nations World Conference on Women, Beijing (paragraph 11) at: http://www.womenpriests.org/church/Beijing.htm
4. Sally M. Vance-Trembath, 'John Paul II's *Ut Unum Sint* and Conversation With Women', *Theological Studies*, 60, 1999, p. 103.
5. 'Letter to Women' (n.3), paragraph 5.
6. BBC News, 'Jail Crisis for Dowry Crimes', 1 June 2000 at: http://news.bbc.co.uk/hi/english/south_asia/newsid_772000/772896.stm
7. The Asia-Pacific NGO (non-governmental organization) Position Paper prepared for the 45th Session of the UN Commission on Status of Women (CSW), New York, 6–16 March 2001 as well as the recent World Conference Against Racism, Racial Discrimination, Xenophobia and Related Intolerance (WCAR), Durban, South Africa, 31 August – 7 September 2001. It was originally drafted by the Asia Pacific Forum on Women, Law and Development (APWLD) based in Chiangmai, Thailand, in consultation with women's NGOs and other grassroots organizations in the Asia-Pacific at:http://194.78.216.158/whrnet3/wcar/key_docs/intersection.htm
8. *New Straits Times Press*, (Kuala Lumpur, Malaysia) 18 August 1998, p. 20.
9. Lynn P. Freedman, 'The Challenge of Fundamentalisms', *Reproductive Health Matters*, No.8, November 1996, p. 56.
10. BBC News, 'China's Unwanted Girls', 23 August 2001 at: http://news.bbc.co.uk/hi/english/world/asia-pacific/newsid_1506000/1506469.stm

11. Chung (n.2), p.103.
12. Arvind P. Nirmal, 'Toward a Christian Dalit Theology', in *Frontiers in Asian Christian Theology: Emerging Trends*, ed. R. S. Sugirtharajah, New York 1994, pp. 40, 34.
13. Alfred T. Hennelly, *Liberation Theology: A Documentary History*, New York 1990, pp.160–1.
14. Jojo M. Fung SJ, *Shoes-Off Barefoot We Walk: A Theology of Shoes-Off*. Kuala Lumpur 1992, p. 79.
15. Wong Wai Ching, 'Negotiating for a Postcolonial Identity: Theology of "the poor woman" in Asia', *Journal of Feminist Studies in Religion*, Fall 2000, 16(2), p. 9.
16. beng hui, 'Time's Up! Moving Sexuality Rights in Malaysia into the New Millennium', *Women in Action*, 1999 at: http://www.isiswomen.org/wia/wia199/sex00006.html
17. United Nations, *The Beijing Declaration and the Platform For Action, Fourth World Conference on Women, Beijing, China, 4–15 September 1995*, paragraph 96.
18. Geeta Rao Gupta, 'Gender, Sexuality and HIV/AIDS: The What, the Why, and the How', Plenary address, XIIth International AIDS Conference, Durban, South Africa, 12 July 2000.
19. Celeste Cinco, 'Virginity in the 90s: Young Filipinas Face up to Contending Pressures [of] Virginity', *Women in Action*, 1999 at: http://www.isiswomen.org/wia/wia199/sex00008.html
20. Young-Hee Shim, 'Gender and Body Politics in Korea: Focusing on the Making of the Feminine Body', *Asian Women*, June 1998, Vol. 6, p. 23.
21. *The New York Times*, 'Mock Tribunal for Sex Slaves Opens', December 2000 at: http://194.78.216.158/whrnet3/tribunal/press/sex_slaves.htm
22. BBC News, 'Vietnam: West is Best for Beauty', 11 January 1999 at: http://news.bbc.co.uk/hi/english/world/asia-pacific/newsid_250000/250630.stm and 'Joyous Homecoming for Acid Attack Victims', 22 July 1999 at: http://news.bbc.co.uk/hi/english/world/south_asia/newsid_401000/401093.stm
23. Chung (n.2), pp. 39, 47.
24. Ibid., pp. 42–3.
25. Ibid., p. 62.
26. Ibid., pp. 63–4. Wong Wai Ching cautions that such postcolonial discourse which polarizes Western imperialist/Asian colonized in politicizing Christ's salvific mission, runs the risk of 'normalisation and routinization of one kind of women's experience – that is, as victims of foreign and home exploitation – and one form of women's agency – that is, as national-liberation combatants'. Wong (n.15), p. 21.
27. Chung (n.2), p. 60.

Mixed-Race Body, Cosmic Race

CARMIÑA NAVIA VELASCO

When, at the beginning of this new millennium, we pause to think about our body, we are faced with an unavoidable reality: our corporeality has been relegated so often throughout the course of our life that it is difficult now to bring it out, to look at it, to concentrate on it. We experience our body, and sometimes we suffer it, without much attention or understanding, without complicity, without any love. Men's and women's bodies are today ignored or interfered with, subjected to pressure, to business, colonized . . . and often humiliated. They are bodies that are not taken into account, either by institutions or in the general social organization of life. 'What bodies do policies consider? From what bodies is politics devised? Which are the power centres that define what policies are for which bodies? How do policies condition bodies so that the latter suit the former?'[1]

I. History and rape

A glance at the greater part of any Latin American city will tell us that our Latin American bodies are *mestizo*, mixed-race bodies, bodies in which different blood lines – black, white, indigenous – meet and mix. These bloods and these traditions have become one in the bodies of most of the men and women of Latin America, and so the result is the mixed-race body. We can equally well say that this mixed-race body is a body that has been silenced: it is not spoken of; it does not speak because it is afraid, or because it looks the other way.

In a more authentic indigenous tradition, the body is taken on and experienced as something natural – its appearances, its cycles, its sicknesses or pleasures form part of nature and are received and understood as such. In a black tradition, the body is the expression of life, its power, in the end life itself: black bodies are a channel of life and show themselves, express themselves, contemplate themselves as such. When this indigenous or black flesh is mixed with white, the body loses some colour, loses its bearings. The white body has so often been repressed . . . commercialized so many other times; the white body – especially the white man's body – has become the master and on its journey has trampled on its brother bodies, black and indigenous. This is why this mixed-race body does not know where to put itself, where it can find itself.

We start from one fact: the human and/or social body is not something outside history, laid down once and for all; it is, on the contrary, something that is developed, that we build up every day, so that '. . . the history of the human body is not so much the succession of different definitions as the narration of its means of development. Definitions cast us back to a body outside history . . . while narration of the body places us facing history, facing the different forms in which the body has been developed and – why not? – lived.'[2]

The question then is how our mixed-race body has been developed and how we are developing it today, on the margins of globalization. Our body registers in its memory and carries in its living, acting flesh the story of its development – the sorrows, humiliations, pleasures and joys that have woven the fabric of our story. In this sense we cannot forget or ignore the fact that our mixed-race body is a body born of rape. The meeting of races that takes place on our land is a violent meeting: our mothers, black and indigenous, are raped or abused by the white conqueror . . . and the mixed-race body is born from this rape. Octavio Paz calls us 'children of the whipped'.[3]

This first rape, like all rapes, leaves its imprint on our Latin American bodies, which awaken to life with mixed feelings made up of hatred and rebellion, fear and suffering. Our body is then a fearful body, ashamed of itself, that hides itself and conceals . . . a body desirous of concealing its origins, anxious to wipe out this fault inscribed in its flesh and blood. But at the same time it is a seeking body, a body that needs to discover itself and proclaim itself in order thereby to achieve its identity and find its place.

This rape worked itself through in a radical colonization: the law, the state, politics, morality, the family, tradition, the church – the whole mixed-race public body was colonized. And all the time, the man's body colonized the woman's body. Colonization changed without coming to an end: fashion, publicity, money, seduction – processes and interests that looked towards the Latin American body in order to capture it, to subdue it, to empty it out and fill it up again. And in the midst of beauty contests and gyms, of dishes and diets, of anorexias and muscles, of aesthetic and deconstructive ideas . . . our men's and women's bodies in search of themselves became a road along on which they continued to look for themselves.

The roads the men and women of our continent have travelled in search of their corporeality are very complex and cannot be simplified:

> The discourse of human beings as bodies understood as history and narration escapes us in the attempt to reduce them to biological, psychological, social or volitional processes, since these human beings as beings-in-the-world, in-relationship . . . become enigmatic and mysterious, and it is just this that always remains to be explained, as though one were dealing with the plot of a good novel, in which the thread on which it hangs together and around which the characters take on life is discovered gradually but can never be clear at the beginning. This plot is woven by the threads that give shape to corporeality.[4]

The history of the shackles on the mixed-race body is, then, a long one. I cannot expand here on this history with its changes and developments. I want just to look at three threads that run right through it: the distorting mirror, the double destruction of women's bodies, the potentialities of the mixed-race body.

II. The foreign model

Let us look at what I call the distorting mirror. While the mirror's complicity helped to hide and so protect the black body and the indigenous body with their partly hidden or sleeping possibilities, the mixed-race body found no space in which to defend itself and did not know where to look, because its model was always a distorting mirror, a borrowed, or rather an imposed model. The Latin American body had to look at other bodies: North American and European ones, bodies that did not show it the way it should take, and today, in the era of so-called globalization, it continues seeing its reflection and its dreams in these other bodies, which are not its other half but an imposed presence.

In the process of inculturation, learning to experience one's body after the manner of rich white people (from Europe and North America) was fundamental. The fashion models: clothes, manners, weights and measures . . . were established by the upper classes who in turn took them from their journeys or magazines. On this route, a body was accepted, was connected, to the extent that it adjusted to what was required. In his study of fashion, Barthes states: 'As for the human body, Hegel had already suggested that it had a relationship of signification with clothing: insofar as it is sentient, pure, the body cannot signify; *clothing signifies the passage from the sentient to the sensed*; it is if you like the signified *par excellence* . . .' And speaking of the function of mannequins (of models, that is), he continues: 'Their essential function is not aesthetic, they are there to present not a beautiful body, subject to canon laws of plastic success, but a body deformed in order to comply with a particular formal generality, that is to say a structure.'[5]

So by guaranteeing one way of living, dressing, or discovering and dreaming the body, the existence of a subjected mixed-race body has always been assured – and is still assured through television models.

III. The destroyed female body

In our cultures the body clearly neither has been nor is experienced in the same way by men as by women. If exclusion and domination have affected one thing above all, this is women's bodies. The female body has always been made the object and means of domestication. From the very instant of our brutal birth as nations, the bodies of black and indigenous women have always provoked a mixture of fear and rejection, of anxiety and attraction, in white men and women. So in so far as the bodies of mixed-race women share in this nature, they must be domesticated. The church, the family, schools, morality, and fashion have all conributed to this task.

There has been an attempt to rub out the female body, to neutralize its diabolical powers, its capacity for sin. The female body became the main focus for all men's anxieties, and on account of this it has has been and still is punished in many ways: 'So a woman has continually to undergo so many subtle humiliations, simply on account of being a woman, that she has developed a sort of deafness, so as not take any notice. Her body is often so humiliated by her surroundings – people or media – that she has learned to do what no other being in the world is capable of doing, or rather what no other being has had to do: gradually to forget her own sexual identity.'[6]

In this context of suffering and humiliation women have undergone, we should bear in mind that:

> The feelings contained in the depths of the body contribute to the developments of certain bodily patterns. These patterns are all learnt. In a certain sense we have received our body, as it is the form and pattern of the movements that reflect the pressure of external events. Sometimes, we need to hold on to feelings of sexual violence in our most hidden depths. Those who have survived a trauma of this kind develop characteristic bodily patterns; they have incorporated the sexual trauma and the attack undergone into their own bodies. Their bodies express not only their

response to the trauma but also the system of self-reliance this has produced.[7]

This is why women have so often expressed and experienced their personalities through sickness. Psychoanalysis even created a concept to describe this mainly female problem: hysteria. In a desperate attempt to defend their bodies from the death decreed by society and morality, women become ill, develop symptoms that isolate them and protect them in this isolation. This, however, has not been sufficient: female flesh, female life even, has to be punished. This is why most of the novels written in Latin America between 1870 and 1910 end with the death of their leading female characters. The heroines of Latin American novels die: they die from sickness – tuberculosis, leprosy, epilepsy; they die murdered, abandoned, suicides. These novels are a clear parable of the impossibility of life for women in a patriarchal society.

These deaths are the product of the ferocity shown by our social system to women's bodies, especially to those of mixed-race women. We must hope that women will begin to think for themselves, so that novels and society will slowly begin to change.

IV. Mixed-race body/cosmic race

It seems worth dwelling a little on the potentialities our mixed-race Latin American body has for the present and the future. We are, fortunately, starting this new millennium with a new attitude to the human body in general, an attitude of reconciliation, tenderness, and love. This new attitude may, then, help us to care for and rescue those bodies most wounded, most abused by life.

In Latin America, we are in a special position to develop a new culture and a new history of the body. This is because our mixed-race body contains all the potential of the three races: the black race at peace with its corporeality; the Indian race in permanent communion with nature, with Pachamama; the white race with its technological and medical advances. If we succeed in producing an exchange among cultures that stems from a mutual embrace of bodies and not from rape or imposition, we shall have brought about the birth of the cosmic race of which Vasconcelos speaks.

The mixed-race body would then be the pre-eminent body in the new situation, the rescued body of the new ethics, an ethics of happiness in accordance with Esperanza Guisán's proposal: 'The concept of *justice as happiness* refers precisely to the development of structures that would guarantee that all men (and all women) receive the information and the freedom they need to devise their own life-plan and that, likewise, they obtain the means necessary to satisfy their needs of every kind, from the most material, such as housing, clothing, food, sex, and the like to needs such as affection, dignity, and so on.[8]

The ethics of happiness would be an ethics of bodies, because a happiness that does not take account of the actual, day-by-day bodies of men and women, young people and children, is unthinkable. In such a setting, the mixed-race body can, in the very near future, bring the information and dreams of its three great roots together in its flesh, as well as their potentials for making those dreams reality.

Translated by Paul Burns

Notes

1. Josefina Hurtado, 'Del cuerpo derecho a los derechos de los cuerpos,' *Revista Conspirando, Cuerpo y Política*, September 2000, Santiago de Chile.
2. María José López Perez, 'Cuerpo, sexo y mujer en la perspectiva de las antropologías' in Mercedes Navarro (ed.), *Para Comprender el Cuerpo de la Mujer, Una perspectiva Bíblica y Etica*, Estella 1996.
3. Octavio Paz develops this theme of rape extensively in his *El laberinto de la soledad*.
4. Josefina Hurtado, art. cit.
5. Roland Barthes, *Sistema de la moda*, Barcelona 1978.
6. Alessandra Bocchetti, *Lo que quiere una mujer*, Madrid 1995.
7. Carolyn J. Braddock, *Las voces del cuerpo*, Bilbao 1999.
8. Esperanza Guisán, 'Razón y pasión en ética' in *Los dilemas de la ética contemporánea*, Barcelona 1990.

Contributors

REGINA AMMICHT-QUINN studied Catholic theology and German. She is a lecturer in theological ethics at the Theological Faculty of the University of Tübingen and the Interfaculty Centre for Ethics in Science, Tübingen. Her publications include: *Von Lissabon bis Auschwitz. Zum Paradigmawechsel in der Theodizeefrage*, Freiburg 1992; *Körper, Religion und Sexualität. Theologische Reflexion zur Ethik der Geschlechter*, Mainz ²2000; *Kultur des Lebens. Bemerkungen zu einer christlichen Anthropologie der Zukunft*, Hildesheimer Texte 2, Hildesheim 2001.

Address: Humboldtstrasse 1, D-60318 Frankfurt am Main, Germany

ELSA TAMEZ was born in Mexico in 1950 and received her Doctor's degree in Theology from the University of Lausanne, Switzerland. She received her Licenciate in Theology in 1979 from the Latin American Biblical Seminary, and received a Licenciate in Literature and Linguistics at the National University of Costa Rica in 1986. She is a faculty member of the Latin American Biblical University in Costa Rica and a member of the team of researchers of the Ecumenical Department of Investigation (DEI) in Costa Rica. Among her publications are: *Diccionario conciso Griego-Español* (1978); *Bible of the Oppressed* (1982), published in Spanish, English, Portuguese, French and Dutch; *The Scandalous Message of James* (1989), published in Spanish, Portuguese and English; *Amnesty of Grace* (1993), published in Spanish, English and German and *When the Horizons Close: Rereading Ecclesiastes* (2000), published in Spanish and English. She has also edited: *Against Machismo* (1987), published in Spanish and English; *Women's Rereading of the Bible* (1988), published in Spanish and English and *Through Her Eyes; Women Theologians from Latin America* (1989) published in Spanish and English.

Address: Universidad Bíblica Latinoamericana, Apartado 901–1000, San José, Costa Rica

HILLE HAKER, who was born in 1962, is academic assitant to the chair of ethics and social ethics at the Catholic Theological Faculty of the University of Tübingen. She is a member of the interfaculty centre for ethics in the sciences, where among other things she was academic co-ordinator for the European Network for Biomedical Ethics in 1989–99. Her most important current publications cover the focal point of her work: literature and ethics (her dissertation was *Moralische Identität. Literarische Lebensgeschichten als Medium ethischer Reflexion*, Tübingen 1999) and biomedical ethics: *The Ethics of Genetics in Human Procreation*, Aldershot 2000 (ed. with Deryck Beyleveld). Her Habilitationsschrift on the Ethics of Human Genetics will appear shortly.

Address: Biesingerstrasse 14, 72070 Tübingen, Germany
E-mail: Hille.Haker@uni-tuebingen.de

KLAUS WIEGERLING was born in Ludwigshafen in 1954. He studied philosophy, comparative religion and ethnology in Mainz, gaining his doctorate in 1983 and his Habilitation in 2001. He writes and lectures on philosophy, information technology and film at the universities of Kaiserslautern, Stuttgart, Mainz, Landau and Linz and the media college in Stuttgart. Along with many articles he has written *Husserls Begriff der Potentialität*, Bonn 1984; *Die Erzählbarkeit der Welt*, Lebach 1989 and *Medienethik*, Stuttgart 1998.

Address: Pirmasenser Strasse 92, D-67655 Kaiserslautern, Germany
E-mail: Wiegerlingklaus@aol.com

CHRISTINA VON BRAUN was born in Rome in 1944. She studied in the USA in Germany. From 1969 to 1981 she lived in Paris as a free-lance author and film-maker and from 1993 she was fellow at the Cultural Institute in Essen and visiting professor in the universities of Frankfurt, Vienna, Klagenfurt, Constance, Innsbruck und Columbia University, New York. Since 1994 she has been Professor of Cultural Sciences at the Humboldt University in Berlin. She has made around fifty films and television programmes on cultural themes and written numerous books and articles on the relationship between gender roles and the history of ideas. These include *Der Ewige Judenhaß. Christlicher Antijudaismus, deutschnationale Judenfeindlichkeit, rassistischer Antisemitismus*, Berlin 2000 and *Versuch über den Schwindel. Religion, Schrift, Bild, Geschlecht*, Zürich and Munich 2001.

Address: Humboldt-Universität zu Berlin, Kulturwissenschaftliches Seminar, Sophienstrasse 22a, 10178 Berlin, Germany, E-mail: CvBraun@culture.hu-berlin.de

ROSEMARY RADFORD RUETHER is a Roman Catholic eco-feminist theologian. She is the Georgia Harkness Professor of Applied Theology at the Garrett-Evangelical Theological Seminary and a member of the graduate faculty of Northwestern University in Evanston, Illinois, USA. She is author or editor thirty-five books and numerous articles on the relationship between theology, feminism, ecology and social justice.

Address: Garrett Evangelical Theological Seminary, 2121 Sheridan Road, Evanston, Illinois 60201, USA
E-mail: rosemary.ruether@nwu.edu

SALLIE MCFAGUE is Carpenter Professor of Theology Emerita, Vanderbilt University Divinity School, where she taught for thirty years. She is at present Distinguished Theologian in Residence at the Vancouver School of Theology in British Columbia. She is the author of several books in the area of Christianity and ecology, especially *Models of God*, *The Body of God*, and most recently, *Life Abundant: Rethinking Theology and Economy for a Planet in Peril*.

Address: Vancouver School of Theology, 600 Iona Drive, Vancouver, BC, V6T 1L4 Canada
E-mail: smcfague@vst.edu

JEAN-GUY NADEAU was born in 1950. He is Professor of Practical Theology in the theology faculty of the University of Montreal and a former president of the International Society of Practical Theology (1995–98). His books include: *L'interprétation, un défi de l'action pastorale*, Montreal 1987; *La prostitution, une affaire de sens*, Montreal 1989; *Dieu en ville. Evangiles et Eglises dans l'espace urbain*, Ottawa, Paris, Geneva and Brussels 1998; and *La théologie, pour quoi, pour qui?*, Montreal 2000.

Address: Faculté de théologie, Université de Montréal, C.P. 6128 Succ. Centre-ville, Montreal, Canada H3C 3J7
E-mail: Jean-Guy.Nadeau@umontreal.ca

Contributors

TINA BEATTIE was born in Lusaka, Zambia in 1955 and now lives in Bristol, UK, with her husband and children. She studied theology at the University of Bristol, and gained her doctorate on Marian Theology and Symbolism in 1999. She currently teaches courses in humanities and world religions with the Open University, while continuing to write and lecture in theology on a freelance basis. Her most recent publications include *Eve's Pilgrimage: A Woman's Quest for the City of Rome*, London and New York 2002 and *God's Mother, Eve's Advocate: a feminist reclamation of Marian Theology and Symbolism*, London and New York 2002 (forthcoming).

Address: 109 Cranbrook Road, Bristol BS6 7DA
E-mail: tinabeattie@btinternet.com

NANCY CARDOSO PEREIRA has a doctorate in Bible studies. She is a Methodist pastor working with the Pastoral Land Commission in Brazil.

Address: Av. Luciano Guidotti 1350, ap. 331, 3424–540
Piracicaba - SP/Brazil
E-mail: nancycp@uol.com.br

RAINER BUCHER was born in Nuremberg in 1956. He studied German and theology in Freiburg im Breisgau and Würzburg, where he gained his doctorate in fundamental theology. From 1986 to 1990 he was assistant to the chair of church history and patrology in the Catholic theological faculty of the University of Bamberg, and from 1991 to1998 he worked at Cusanuswerk, the study centre sponsored by the Geram bishops. He gained his Habilitation in pastoral theology in Bamberg in 1996 and was appointed Professor of Pastoral Theology and Kerygmatics there in 1999. Since 2000 he has been Director of the Institute of Pastoral Theology and Pastoral Psychology in the University of Graz. His publications include: *Nietzsches Mensch und Nietzsches Gott. Das Spätwerk als philosophisch-theologisches Programm*, Frankfurt am Main, Bern and New York 1986, ²1993; *Kirchenbildung in der Moderne. Eine Untersuchung der Konstitutionsprinzipien der deutschen katholischen Kirche im 20. Jahrhundert*, Stuttgart 1998.

Address: Parkstrasse 1, A-8010 Graz, Austria
E-mail: R.Bucher@t-online.de

Contributors

FARIDEH AKASHE-BÖHME was born in Iran and studied German, history, politics and sociology in Frankfurt and Darmstadt. She gained her doctorate in sociology. Her publications include: *In geteilten Welten. Fremdheitserfahrungen zwischen Migration und Partizipation*, Frankfurt 2000; *Die Burg von Char Barrdi. Von Persien nach Deutschland – die Geschichte einer Jugend*, Frankfurt 2000; *Die islamische Frau ist anders*, Gütersloh 1997; *Frausein – Fremdsein*, Frankfurt ²1994; *Die Darstellung der iranischen Revolution in der bundesrepublikanischen Presse*, Göttingen 1986.

Address: Rosenhöhweg 25, 64287 Darmstadt
E-mail: gboehme@hrzpub.tu-darmstadt.de

SYLVIA MARCOS is Visiting Professor of Mesoamerican Religions at the School of Religions of Claremont Graduate University. She has been Visiting Luce Professor at Union Theological Seminary and has taught at Harvard Divinity School. She has lectured widely, especially in Latin America. She is senior researcher of the permanent seminar on Gender and Anthropology at Instituto de Investigaciones Antropologicas of the National Autonomous University of Mexico. She has done extensive field studies and action-research with grassroots indigenous healers and women political activists where her historical research has been validated by contemporary data from the field. Her latest book is *Gender/Bodies/Religions*. She is co-editor of *Chiapas: el Factor* Religioso, and is currently co-editing *Towards a New Feminist Imaginary*.

E-mail: smarcos@infosel.net.mx

GOSBERT T. M. BYAMUNGU is a Catholic professor, holding the chair of Biblical Hermeneutics at the Ecumenical Institute of Bossey of the World Council of Churches in Switzerland. He is a Catholic priest from Tanzania, and holds a doctorate in biblical theology from the Pontifical Gregorian University in Rome. He is author of *Stronger Than Death: Reading David's Rise for Third Millennium*, Rome 1996 and has pastoral and professional experience in Africa, Europe and the USA.

Address: Ecumenical Institute, 2, Chemin Chenevière, Bogis-Bossey, CH-1298 Cèligny, Geneva, Switzerland
E-mail: gst@wcc-coe.org

Contributors

SHARON A. BONG is a PhD candidate with the Department of Religious Studies, Lancaster University, UK. Her ten-year involvement with the women's movement in Malaysia encompasses activism at national, regional and international levels. As a former journalist with the *New Straits Times Press*, she also lectured for the Gender Studies Programme at the University of Malaya and worked as a programme officer with the Asian-Pacific Resource & Research Centre for Women, Kuala Lumpur, Malaysia. She was part of the Malaysian contingent to the NGO Forum in Huairou which preceded the 1995 Fourth UN World Conference on Women, China. She has contributed to the *Catholic Asian News* and *In God's Image*. Her main interests ares women's/human rights, cultures and religions.

Address: Department of Religious Studies, Lancaster University, Lancaster LA1 4YG
E-mail: bongsa@hotmail.com

CARMIÑA NAVIA VELASCO is Professor of Literature at the Universidad del Valle in Colombia; she also lectures in linguistics and theology and is co-founder and director of the Centro Cultural Popular Meléndez of Cali, her birthplace. Her books include: *El dios que nos revelan las mujeres*, Bogotá 1998; *La ciudad interpela la biblia*, Quito 2001.

Address: Calle 2a B No. 94–20 Barrio El Jordán, Apartado Aéreo 25152, Cali, Colombia
E-mail: cnaviav@emcali.net.co

CONCILIUM

FOUNDERS

A. van den Boogaard
P. Brand
Y. Congar OP †
H. Küng
J.-B. Metz
K. Rahner SJ †
E. Schillebeeckx OP

FOUNDATION

Jan Peters SJ, President
Hermann Häring
Regina Ammicht-Quinn
Christoph Theobald SJ
Ellen van Wolde
Ben van Baal, Treasurer

DIRECTORS

Regina Ammicht-Quinn
María Pilar Aquino Vargas
Christophe Boureux OP
Seán Freyne
Hermann Häring
Hille Haker
Maureen Junker-Kenny
Karl-Josef Kuschel
Alberto Melloni
Teresa Okure SHCJ
Elisabeth Schüssler Fiorenza
Jon Sobrino SJ
Janet Martin Soskice
Luiz Carlos Susin OFMCap.
Elsa Tamez
Christoph Theobald SJ
Miklós Tomka
Felix Wilfred
Ellen van Wolde

General Secretariat: Erasmusplein 1, 6525 HT Nijmegen, The Netherlands
http://www.concilium.org
Manager: Baroness Christine van Wijnbergen

Concilium Subscription Information

Issues published in 2002

February	2002/1: *The Many Voices of the Bible* Edited by Seán Freyne and Ellen van Wolde
April	2002/2: *The Body and Religion* Edited by Regina Ammicht-Quinn and Elsa Tamez
June	2002/3: *Brazil* Edited by J. Oscar Beozzo and L. C. Susin
October	2002/4: *Religious Education of Boys and Girls* Edited by Werner Jeanrond and Lisa Sowle Cahill
December	2002/5: *The Rights of Women* Edited by María Pilar Aquino Vargas and Elisabeth Schüssler Fiorenza

New subscribers: to receive Concilium 2002 (five issues) anywhere in the world, please copy this form, complete it in block capitals and send it with your payment to the address below.

Please enter my subscription for Concilium 2002

☐ Individual   **£25.00**/*US$50.00*   ☐ Institutional   **£35.00**/*US$75.00*

Issues are sent by air to the USA; please add £10/US$20 for airmail dispatch to all other countries (outside Europe).

☐ I enclose a cheque payable to SCM-Canterbury Press Ltd for £/$ ....

☐ Please charge my MasterCard/Visa   Expires ....

................./................./................./................

Signature ....

Name/Institution ....

Address ....

....

....

Telephone ....

Concilium   SCM Press   9–17 St Albans Place   London N1 0NX   England
Telephone (44) 20 7359 8033   Fax (44) 20 7359 0049
E-mail: scmpress@btinternet.com

www.ingramcontent.com/pod-product-compliance
Lightning Source LLC
Chambersburg PA
CBHW070643300426
44111CB00013B/2241